NERVOUS SYSTEMS

Books by Sara Billups

Orphaned Believers

Nervous Systems

NERVOUS SYSTEMS

Spiritual Practices to Calm Anxiety in Your Body, the Church, and Politics

SARA BILLUPS

BakerBooks
a division of Baker Publishing Group
Grand Rapids, Michigan

Published by Baker Books
a division of Baker Publishing Group
Grand Rapids, Michigan
BakerBooks.com

Printed in the United States of America

Library of Congress Cataloging-in-Publication Data
Names: Billups, Sara, 1978– author
Title: Nervous systems : spiritual practices to calm anxiety in your body, the church, and politics / Sara Billups.
Description: Grand Rapids, Michigan : Baker Books, a division of Baker Publishing Group, [2025] | Includes bibliographical references.
Identifiers: LCCN 2024059580 | ISBN 9781540904218 paperback | ISBN 9781540905161 casebound | ISBN 9781493451098 ebook
Subjects: LCSH: Anxiety—Religious aspects—Christianity | Worry—Religious aspects—Christianity | Spiritual formation
Classification: LCC BV4908.5 .B497 2025 | DDC 242/.4—dc23/eng/20250709
LC record available at https://lccn.loc.gov/2024059580

Cover design by Jake Nicolella

The author is represented by the literary agency of The Bindery Agency, www.TheBinderyAgency.com.

Some names and details have been changed to protect the privacy of the individuals involved.

Baker Publishing Group publications use paper produced from sustainable forestry practices and postconsumer waste whenever possible.

25 26 27 28 29 30 31 7 6 5 4 3 2 1

For Sue

When you are a child who believes your brain can keep planes from crashing, it's imaginative and precocious. When you're an adult who thinks your own churning mind is what keeps everything safe, it's called anxious.

Mary Laura Philpott, *Bomb Shelter*

Contents

PART THREE: THE BODY POLITIC

Introduction

My father and my father's father were anxious. I was worried over before I was born. I came into this world with that inheritance. A bottle-fed meal of inherited and observed anxiety. Then I took what I'd been given and made it my own.

Everyone I know is worried about something, and most of the Christians I know find little comfort in Jesus's words in the Sermon on the Mount, "Do not worry" (Matt. 6:25) like a bird or a flower.

Jesus, stop pouring salt on the wound, we might think. *Stop making it sound so easy. Clearly you didn't live in a time like we do, in a mental health crisis and through several geopolitical conflicts and a global pandemic, which only calcified our differences.* As Krista Tippett said about the years we're living through, "You could make an argument that our entire societal nervous system was stressed."[1]

If Jesus said to not worry, I believe he meant it. But two thousand years later, I could not experience peace. This pain point—the dissonance between the head reading "do not worry" and the heart worrying—was the one I wanted to understand.

I began to think about the question culturally, as a Christian considering her place in the American church and the local congregation. Like many of us, I want to see what is broken in the church—and America—healed. But we're far from where we want to be.

And so, I began to read. Studying recent reporting and cultural analysis, and even my own unpublished journals, I set out to understand the cultures and stereotypes swaying American Christian identity so that I could try to find and offer hope in the face of personal anxieties and the anxieties of our frenetic culture.

How Did We Get Here?

In *A Non-Anxious Presence*, author and pastor Mark Sayers writes that as technology expands, anxiety follows, affecting us personally and collectively. "Just as the modern world brings technological breakthroughs, advancements in science, and greater individual freedoms, it also creates anxiety. Anxiety is viewed as an individual ailment, and indeed many experience it as such. However . . . there is a structural element to anxiety."[2]

Sayers points to the Industrial Revolution as an example. "As the world in the nineteenth century took its first technological steps to become a global village, anxiety birthed a whole raft of new and previously never before encountered illnesses. . . . Men suffered from what was named 'brain fevers,' 'brainstorms,' and 'nervous exhaustions.'"[3] Women were diagnosed with the gendered "hysteria." The market responded, Sayers writes, including the beginning of self-help, and "rests, retreats, vegetarianism, and vacations rushed into vogue among those suffering from suffocating anxiety. Yet little seemed to work."[4]

The pandemic was its own revolution, not one in which we industrialized but rather were decommissioned. It could have been different.

The Australian musician and writer Nick Cave says the pandemic was a window where things might have gotten better, "but we blew it. We squandered it. Early on, many of us felt that a chance was presented to us, as a civilisation, to put aside our vanities, grievances and divisions, our hubris, our callous disregard for each other, and come together around a common enemy. . . . To our shame this didn't happen. The Right got scarier, the Left got crazier, and our already fractured civilisation atomised into something that resembled a collective lunacy."[5]

My own collective lunacy got loonier and sadder and more melancholic during the pandemic. The night we knew Covid was here felt like we had moved into a haunted house. We pretended the noises were explainable for a week or two. Then the apparition, the phase beyond denial. We saw the Covid ghost in Seattle before other parts of the country. I panicked and called a calm friend in Michigan from the upstairs bathroom. I had asthma. I had old and ill parents. I had kids that needed to learn during the day while I worked.

A group of PTA moms had gathered at the park earlier in the week and predicted school would close for the rest of the year. They were forming some sort of co-op learning pod, and I was asked for my email. "You're joking," I said. I had the old feeling that I was missing something. School would just be canceled for a few days, I was certain. But the night I called my friend, I felt foolish for being in the fog of denial a couple of days longer than my neighbors. I sat on the bathroom floor and prayed with her, and somehow her being OK made me less claustrophobic.

Then George Floyd was killed. And my husband, Drew, heard a story of a mother whose son had been given "The Talk" before even a sex talk, but he had been splayed across a police car at twelve anyway. Drew is not a crier. He came upstairs weeping.

Writer Sofia Onte said, "Truth is, I'm tired."[6] As white people living middle-class lives in a white-led world, Drew and I were not trying to pretend we understood the weariness of a person of color. Instead, we were always on the precipice of crying in those months as the depth of the racism we didn't know was in our hearts surfaced. On June 5, 2020, our local station KEXP aired eight minutes and forty-six seconds of silence at 8:46 a.m. to represent the number of minutes and seconds it was initially reported that George Floyd's neck was crushed. We sat on the couch and listened to the silence, the kids in a stream of light. My son's hair looked even blonder then.

Instead of feeling anxious, for a little while during the summer of America's racial reckoning I was buoyed by the need to "get to work," personally and collectively. But it didn't take long until I slipped back into an ambiguous worry. A generalized sense that the color, slant of light, and posture of my motivation to do something was off. Misaligned.

I watched Black Lives Matter protests over my phone on the porch that summer, in the dark next to the screen. The big trees and clean air were still as I saw braver people get tear-gassed in Seattle's Capitol Hill neighborhood. I wondered if I should go downtown. I didn't know where to place the heaving worry that kept my hands holding a small screen. I was taught how to worry, I realized, but not how to protest. My heart wanted to be there, but in my anxiety, all I could see were green comic-book poofs of coronavirus, like neon clouds hovering over the heads in the crowd.

Then the insurrection, the 2020 election. It was a time I knew we would talk about later. A "where were you when MLK was assassinated" or "when 9/11 happened" series of events. The years 2020 and 2021 felt like history being made, and there was some hope that we could learn from it as it was happening instead of in retrospect. Eventually, the sense that my anxiety could somehow be productive by tapping into a collective move toward social change fizzled in me. It fizzled because I had the luxury of not being burdened with any real threat to my well-being. I was tired, so I took a break because I could. By the time the 2024 election took place, my anxious and exhausted Christian peers and I scrambled to make sense of what could not be denied: America is more deeply divided by party line than anyone wants to believe, and we're facing a dangerous and uncertain future. "Do not worry" sounded less relevant than ever.

Looking for Answers

Maybe you know anxiety well as the buzz in your brain that won't turn off when you're supposed to be asleep.[7] Maybe you know it as the chronic notification checking for the next email, the next "like," or the next headline. Anxiety often includes fear of the unknown.[8] It casts a net into the future, mulling over and catastrophizing about what might happen. Anxiety is primal, the reptilian brain reacting to perceived threats. In a sense, anxiety is a good thing when it is preventative. Anxiety serves us throughout life by warning us, and the idea is not to turn it off but rather to turn the volume knob down to a reasonable level.

Not all eras are anxious like this one. The broader, universal reasons—the rapid expansion of generative AI, the impact of social media on our psyches, the market cloaked as wellness culture—are easy to identify. External stressors are coming at all of us—politics, church, family, and financial stress. But more interesting to me are the reasons why the anxiety they bring gets into our systems and blooms in the first place. What I am trying to understand in these pages is how to be present in an era of pervasive personal and collective anxiety.

My first book, *Orphaned Believers*, looked back on the seismic forces of end-times culture, culture wars, and consumerism in the '80s and '90s and how they shook the American church. In *Nervous Systems*, our vantage point is on the here and now, our current dis-ease. We'll explore how anxiety manifests in three areas—the body, the church body, and the body politic—to better understand its source and find healthy resources in the Christian story that serve as antidotes to personal and systemic worry.

First, the body. This is my story but not my anxiety alone. I wanted to understand both the anxiety we carry in our bodies and in the bodies of people we love. I'll use my own story to compare and contrast with yours around mental and physical health: the anxiety from our family of origin, caregiving for aging parents, and wellness culture.

My son, a young member of Gen Z, began to navigate intrusive thoughts and scrupulosity when he started middle school, and it did not take long for me to see these themes, until then undiagnosed, in myself. I hear about this pattern in stories shared by other parents more and more. One friend received a late-in-life autism diagnosis after her son was diagnosed. Another, ADHD after his kid. And my goodness, are our kids anxious.

A 2023 Deloitte survey of more than twenty-two thousand Gen Z and Millennial respondents found that "nearly half of Gen Zs and four in 10 millennials feel stressed or anxious all or most of the time, with women and other under-represented groups most impacted."[9] A 2023 Gallup and Walton Family Foundation survey found that only 47% of Gen Z reports that they are "thriving in their lives." This is among the lowest percentage across all generations in the U.S.[10] As I read these stats, the faces of kids I've known since they were babies who are struggling as young adults ran through my mind like a photo flip-book.

Second, the church. The American church was a place of stability—or at least carried the myth of stability as the unquestioned center of society—for a long time. That shifted in the 1960s onward, when the center didn't hold. Church leaders became burned out and increasingly sidelined, congregants in the pews felt burned out and sidelined, and the Moral Majority capitalized on those feelings, platforming culture wars to avert our tired eyes. Many pastors and clergy made insular choices to stay in power and cloak abuse motivated by anxiety. And others capitalized on the gut-level worry of their parishioners.

The church is a system causing anxiety and impacting mental health when it should be a place of rest. The radical call of Jesus to live in and not of the world? I began to wonder how we'd gotten it all wrong. Instead of being set apart, we've overcorrected to either withdraw from or immerse ourselves in a Christian culture that is often not really about Jesus but about our quest to be safe and accepted. As a Christian considering her place in the capital-C church and the story of my local congregation, I wanted to understand church anxiety, not to burn down but to build up.

Third, the political. Our anxiety acutely manifests in political polarization. While each generation has had their own flavor of culture war issues and dysfunction in Washington, DC, our current taste is especially sour. The people in the US make up a body politic—a collective group of citizens—that is in turn governed via politicians representing states that are the cherriest red or the inkiest blue. Especially after the 2024 election, I wondered if the brokenness of politics could be less ultimate in our lives while staying engaged and aware of policies and actions that affect people who are marginalized and oppressed.

Bigger Than Us

I've plumbed the forces shaping my anxiety. I recognize that many are familiar and common, like caregiving for elders in a culture that doesn't value them and navigating changes in the body in midlife. Beyond our individual experiences, we all encounter systemic anxiety that comes from various structures and organizations such as evangelicalism, in which I was raised.

There are threats outside the body that our immune system is trying to defend against, but instead, as therapist and rabbi Edwin Friedman says, the immune system "can be perverted to attack the host."[11] Outside threats are systemically overwhelming our cultural immune system, and it isn't working properly. Anxieties particular to evangelicalism may be less familiar to readers who were raised in a different faith tradition or no particular tradition. But you don't have to have grown up in the church or identify as a Christian to understand how the social and political forces within the sanctuary continue to impact our broader cultural moment.

An Invitation to Hope

My parents are trying to keep living in bodies that are failing them. My life is maxed with responsibilities. The world is falling apart. And yet, I am literally less anxious. There is only one explanation. Well, I suppose there could be two. The first may be that I am numbed out, be it from a substance use disorder or a reality television addiction, and I am so numb I am detached. Or the second, which is what I believe to be true, is that instead of clenching down and waiting for the affliction to pass, I have found that God can meet us in the presence of anxiety and change us.

Writer Kate Bowler said, "Most of the things that build our lives are the things that can come apart at any moment."[12] Ah, there it is: The root of my own anxiety is the belief I carry that something could unexpectedly be swept away in an instant—health, ability, life itself.

Maybe you think two things at this point. First, this book will be a real downer. I've attempted to write about personal and systemic anxiety with levity. Not to diminish, but to nourish. Second, I'm writing with my own anxiety, which is and has always been centered around the body, and that is too different from yours. Yours is about a friend maybe, or a kid, or the environment, or the workweek. I worried about that too when I set out to write this book. But I hope I've dug down enough to get to the bottom of the ice-cream tub of worry, and that whatever the flavor, we're both in the same cardboard container. Letting go of the grip of our anxiety, whatever its variety, happens right where we are and is formed by the complexity of our own stories and the world around us.

There are some things that take a long time to pinpoint in ourselves. But when I sat down to write about my anxiety, I discovered the same themes had been circling for months, even years—these questions of the body, the church body, and the body politic—but I was trying to get at them in different ways. Through understanding these major forces impacting my anxiety, I wanted to comprehend some things personal and universal about control, affliction, and ultimately faith.

The more I thought about the personal, the church, and the political anxiety of our era, the more my central tension crystallized: Jesus said to not worry, but it does not seem possible to live in our world free of personal and pervasive systemic anxiety. The two postures—Jesus's calm and our worry—did not seem reconcilable. They weren't, until something changed in my own heart.

In my midforties, I started the Spiritual Exercises, a nine-month-long Ignatian "retreat." The Exercises are traditionally conducted in a month of intense prayer and contemplation; I opted for a modified version of the Exercises centered in an hour of morning prayer. Here, I learned more about the posture of holy indifference, and as I did, I discovered something that I can pass on to you that does not require a month of retreating. I noticed that the more I pried open my hands toward a posture of acceptance, the less I worried.

At first, I pat its head, my burgeoning sense of calm. *You're cute*, this calm feeling, like a scruffy mutt at the back door. Then, the more I read, the further into the Exercises I go, the more I begin to tolerate my anxiety. We go on occasional walks, me and my calm companion. Soon enough, I tap my hand on the bed, and the dog jumps up, sighing and settling. Even in sleep, when before I would wake up with a racing heart, I am more at peace now; a warm body sleeps at my feet.

On a bad night, up and worried, I go to the bathroom and stand under a skylight. The light of the moon is on my hands. I sense God saying, "Moonlight is a different kind of light." Even in the dark, there is a soft, pearly light that is nothing like the sun that throws itself against the wall, the skin.

Jesus said, "Do not worry," and I believe he meant it. To say it plainly: My anxiety did not dissipate. Instead, God met me repeatedly in its very presence.

PART ONE

THE BODY

1

Leans Anxious

My heart at midlife was restless in three places—at least. Its chambers hummed with anxiety: A line drawn straight until the hand holding the pencil trembles. An EKG machine spreadsheeting inky dips after each beat. A seismograph measuring low earthquakes you can feel, but barely. I naturally run at a 2.5 magnitude level of worry, maybe a three.

First, I was anxious about fathers. Men had both helped and harmed me. Church fathers and dads. Heavenly fathers and strange uncles. I grew up with a father who was impulsive but still loving. There were men in the first half of my life whom I wanted to be like, I wanted to be with, and I wanted to avoid. Godly men, dangerous men, bookish men, addicted men.

Second, I was anxious about mothers. Women had both helped and harmed me. I grew up with a mother who could be hot or cold but was usually fun. Once we danced on top of a mold of cherry Jell-O on the kitchen floor. I can still feel the squish. There were women in the first half of my life whom I wanted to look like, I wanted to befriend, and I wanted to avoid. Sunday school women, artistic women, homeschooled women, intellectual women.

Third, I was anxious about supporting my parents and taking care of my kids. I had already learned a thing or two about caregiving by my forties. I had seen the changing shapes, colors, and forms of anxiety that began in childhood and had traced a pencil line from being a daughter, to mothering, to caring for my mother and father. In the first half of my life, I had wanted to untangle from my parents but still nap on their overstuffed couch on the weekend. For a season in my twenties, I'd call on Sundays and see them at Christmas. Eventually, when parenting my own daughter and son, I needed Mom and Dad's help and took as much of it as they could give. When they needed me as they aged, I frequently felt guilty about how often I was not available to them.

Ever-Present Anxiety

Almost seven million adults in the US have generalized anxiety disorder.[1] If we are not anxious, someone we love is probably wrestling with worry. Some of us have experienced anxiety from a young age. Others develop anxiety later in life, be it from a specific inciting incident or a growing, gnawing feeling of dread. Sometimes age gives us more knowledge, technique, and perspective about anxiety, but it also delivers more opportunities for disillusionment.

A 2023 television series called *Lucky Hank* depicts a professor who is flailing in midlife. Hank's college bookstore doesn't carry his book. He has no interest in and, at times, disdains his writing students. He would not join a club that would have him as a member, that old Groucho Marx trope. The series ran for one season before it was canceled. Apparently, there is only so much wallowing a viewer can handle.

In the pilot episode, Hank tells his wife he is typically 80 percent worried or anxious. His wife says most people run at 30 or 40 percent. She says her anxiety is at 30.[2] Their chasm widens. I am closer to Hank than his wife, anxious in perpetuity. I lean anxious. My anxiety is a cocktail of genetic predisposition and learned behavior garnished with a maraschino cherry of cultural anxiety sunk to the bottom of the glass.

Physician and writer Dr. Jen Gunter says that anxiety disorders are as real as any physical condition such as high blood pressure or strep throat.[3] They also make plenty of room for creative thinking. When you are worrying, what does your brain look like? If I could see inside my brain when worrying, I imagine it would be highlighter yellow, maybe Hi-C Ecto Cooler green. Channels in the brain carry a glowing flood of anxiety between the mind and body—lightning in a cloud brain with neon threads of adrenaline.

To calm a heart racing from worry, there are at-home remedies that a Google search will tell you to try. Run an ice cube across your wrists; cold water can shock the senses and lower levels of cortisol, the stress hormone. It's a localized version of pouring a bucket of ice water over the head of a drunk college student. Wake the hell up, kid.

Other remedies you can try: Eat something small and sweet, maybe a piece of hard candy. Grandma candy, like a Werther's Original or Butter Rum LifeSavers. Smell perfume or essential oil, ideally something nostalgic. Breathe in the shape of a box: inhale for five seconds at the top left corner, hold your breath for five to the top right side, exhale down the right side for five seconds, and hold your breath to connect the box to the bottom left corner for the final five; repeat a few times. Take a walk outside.

Anxious Within the Quiet

Sometimes being outside helps me. Other times, I most clearly sense the disquiet within me when it contrasts with nature, though the drive to it often provides a sense of calm. There is a curve on I-90 from Seattle when Mount Si comes into view. I've only climbed to the top once, but I've passed it on the interstate a hundred times. There is something grounding about proportionality, about seeing something larger than your own life for a moment. The grounding I get driving there doesn't last. Walking along a path with leftover patches of snow near the base of Si, I pull up a layer of moss and press my palm into the dirt. Underneath avoidance and distraction, there is a pull toward natural quiet. But when I'm flared, my always-on anxiety is amplified by the stillness instead of soothed by it.

As I hike, as in my everyday life, I worry about wars overseas, national and local politics, issues in my city, the future of the American church, the people in my church, my kids' schools, my two kids. These worries are not random. I have been clinically diagnosed with generalized anxiety, and my fear of uncertainty and lack of control most often manifest in one specific area: health anxiety.

My mind is the ultimate empath that can take information about other people's health issues and re-create their physical symptoms. You should see me in action. I can physically vibrate with worry. My breast hums. My lip hums. If you have restless leg syndrome, I will have it tomorrow. If your head is splitting with a migraine, mine will have a dull ache in a few hours. If your eye flutters like a hummingbird and you comment on it over coffee, I will match your twitch with an optical migraine.

Walking through the woods, I ask myself who I would be without anxiety. Would I recognize myself? Would the absence of anxiety be a clear gain? Or would it also represent the loss of something in me I don't really want to be without?

I once jotted down something my spiritual director, Dan, said in a session about my shadow side. Long before Dan mentioned it, Carl Jung, the founder of analytic psychology, wrote about the shadow side, which is the area where emotion is hidden or repressed. Human beings need to understand their shadows in order to become emotionally whole.

During our appointment, Dan said, "Sara, what if anxiety is the shadow side of deep care. If you didn't care, you wouldn't worry." I usually appreciate when a person I trust names something in my life that I can't see for myself. "Yes," I said, thinking about it. "If I wasn't so anxious, I wonder if I would be as faithful to people I love? I also think my creativity is linked to my anxiety; they're different sides of the same coin. If I was not anxious, would I have the same imagination?"

Not Your Thoughts

Sometimes, I am loyal to my anxiety, and in a way, I love it because I have conflated anxiety with myself. We are smashed together, layers of baklava dough collapsed into each other. Break me in two and you could see the lines.

I think about feelings, about how everyone says "we are not what we feel," that we are more than just the sum of our emotions. I partially believe this. To the extent that I do believe it, I'm unclear on how to separate myself from the things I feel.

One possible source of insight presented itself. I read a *Psychology Today* feature called "You Are Not Your Thoughts."[4] The article encourages me to "watch" my thoughts and differentiate the observer, me, from the idea. It occurred to me that maybe the principles in the article apply to both thinking and feeling.

"Try this," the article suggests. "Think, I cannot lift my arms above my head, and while you think this, actually raise your arms above your head (if you are physically capable). Now try this: think, I cannot stand on one leg, and while you think this (again if you are able), stand on one leg. Notice that the connection between thinking and doing is illusory. We can easily think about one thing and do another. . . . Your mind is not in charge. You are!"[5]

I "watch" myself feel unconvinced and awkward after reading the article, the character equivalent of a mom having a midlife crisis listening to a self-help tape in her car. But maybe this thought is not in charge either.

"What's Important to You?"

My anxiety therapist, also named Sara, is one of my favorite people. It's part of some ethics code that you can't be friends with your therapist. If we were real friends, connected outside of a professional therapist-client relationship, she could probably become uncredentialed. So I imagine coming across her at dinner, at a brewery in the Central District, eating fries and drinking an IPA. She is laughing with her husband. He is holding their baby in a carrier, and there is a well-behaved dog at their feet. I wonder what to do in this scenario, and I decide to walk by and quickly smile but not talk to her in real life.

Running into your therapist is like running into a teacher outside of school. Once, I saw my fifth-grade teacher at the drugstore, buying shampoo. And it was unbelievable. Because teachers are in school. Don't they live in school? Maybe there is a cot in the supply room where they sleep? They are our teachers, and they have no business buying shampoo. They are famous to us, the wonderful, tender bosses of us. We are the center of their lives. How can a teacher function without her students?

I would not talk to Sara if I ran into her getting a beer or buying shampoo. Yet I tell her about my darkest corners. Sara and I meet once every few weeks and talk about my health anxiety where I am grateful that I can budget for these regular sessions. I tell her things that I am sure will bring her to a new level of shock and concern. Like, "press the button and sound the alarm, drop the professional lingo about cognitive behavior therapy" concern. The kind of concern that warns her, *This woman is actually freaking nuts.*

Sara tells me to think of the things I could do with my time instead of worrying. "What's important to you? Imagine a future where you're not anxious about your body," she says. "I would spend time with my family and write," I tell her easily.

The idea is to picture how much more spacious life could be if I didn't exhaust exponential energy on anxiety. But that concept implies I can bucket my thoughts like I do activities in my day: go for a jog, write a little, pray. I can assign time slots to those things, thirty-minute brackets. My anxiety is not time-slottable. It is a hum, like the radio always on low while I drive or make dinner. I cannot take the time back that anxiety requires from me because it is meshed into the moments of my day. Jesus said to not worry, to be like the birds and the flowers. That sounds very ambitious; I just wanted a little relief.

Eventually, I began to accept that my thoughts are only things that pass through and can limit as much as free me. But I still could not let go of a sense that my closeness to God hinges on my thinking about God, about whether God is near. My feeling close to God or not close to God is very much about me as the main character. I wonder why I take myself so seriously.

The Gospel of Luke says that when we give good things, good things will be given. In the end, when all things are made well, "a good measure, pressed down, shaken together and running over, will be poured into your lap" (6:38). An abundance of oil from ripe olives. Surely, this is Jesus the redeemer. Jesus the liberator. Jesus the revelator. I read these things and, feelings aside, started to believe them. There are only so many dead ends you reach before you let a little bit go. What a relief to know it was never about us in the first place.

The Myth of Control

By the time I turned forty-five, the low-magnitude rumble of my lifelong anxiety moved into the Big One, a yearslong quake triggered by the health crises of my parents, who are now in their seventies and unwell. My father was diagnosed with a treatable but not curable cancer the first summer of the pandemic and given three and a half years to live based on his age and staging. It has been three years and two months. My mother was diagnosed with Parkinson's disease nine years ago and more recently dementia. She progressed slowly for a long time, but her condition declined quickly once my father received his diagnosis. She began to experience paranoia and psychosis, seeing people who weren't there at all hours of the day. She often saw two Dads. "Isn't one enough?" I asked her once, trying to bring levity to the situation. Her eyes got huge like she was scared. Then, she huffed a little laugh.

My parents are swan diving together, hand in hand, and I would be flattened if I tried to catch their fall. Dad's body is failing, and Mom's mind is failing. Dad's mind was impacted by a stroke that also caused a broken hip two years ago, compounding his cancer with other maladies, including blood clots and mysterious falls that required hospitalization. He's always been anxious, but he had become depressed and lost much of his impulse control. One night Dad woke up and saw someone else in the bathroom, then the mirror. My parents either do not recognize themselves or they multiply themselves.

I am both like and unlike my parents. I chase the myth of control, but I am not outwardly compulsive. I often carry a sense that while nothing is wrong, nothing is truly right. When I was a kid, Dad worried and Mom made things better. Now, I am a mother and can see both of their qualities—worrier and soother—in me as I parent. My anxiety manifests in my body like a weight, and sometimes the pressing of the palm of affliction is heavier than others. At times, I resist. Occasionally, I sense the drag to be horizontal.

Sitting at my desk, I imagine a magnet pulling me off the chair and onto the carpet. In the kitchen, I cook something, but in my mind, I am lying down as I fry an egg. I drive on an errand and imagine a big brass bed on the side of the road with a frilly blanket. It is Stevie Nicks–style, a cinematic bed from the 1970s. I picture myself pulling the car over and crawling under the sheets.

2

Anxious Bodies

We're formed by what we remember and by dispositions that were modeled to us before we could understand them. In my case, a salient model was my parents' worry. I was worried over on train rides between Fort Wayne and Chicago. Worried over at summer barbecues and holiday dinners. Worried over in my bed, in the pew, and at the school desk. Worried over during family vacations to Orlando and New York City. Even fun times are linked with a memory of my parents being apprehensive.

The autonomic nervous system (ANS) is a sort of cruise control for your body. Just as the cruise control in a car manages a set speed without the driver needing to adjust the throttle, the ANS controls all of the things our body does on its own without us thinking about them—for example, our blood pressure, digestion, and breathing. It has three parts: the enteric system, which supports digestion; the parasympathetic system, which calms us and lets us stay at rest; and the sympathetic system, which keeps us safe by alerting us to danger and triggering a fight, flight, freeze, or fawn response.

Psychologist Christine Runyan describes the nervous system as "exquisitely designed. It is a beautiful evolutionary adaptation . . . , if we were to ever lose it, we would become extinct."[1] Runyan explains some of the things that happen to us physically when a threat is sensed so that our nervous system can prepare for danger: Blood is diverted to our muscles, glucose gives more energy, immunity increases, digestion halts, our heart rate gets faster.

At times, I half wonder if my father was born without a parasympathetic nervous system, the part of the ANS that regulates rest. When he's not sleeping, Dad almost constantly presents as being on alert. He is also often symptomatic with one condition or another, his body warning him of threats real or imagined. In the '80s and '90s, Dad's health anxiety thrived without help from Google. He would often leaf through symptoms in an encyclopedia of medical conditions we kept on the top shelf of the closet in the guest room next to a calorie-counting book. Following Dad's lead, I used to pull the encyclopedia down, trying to self-diagnose a bee sting or a stomachache.

When he was otherwise healthy in his thirties, Dad was diagnosed with frequent muscle twitches that were unrelated to any other medical conditions. Years later, I asked him about it once at breakfast, having started to experience my own mysterious muscle spasms in various limbs in my thirties that resulted in a battery of doctor visits and tests. He sounded mildly disgusted that I didn't remember the details of his experience. He could have saved me the trips to the doctor if only I'd asked. He took a bite of waffle and said in a lovingly sarcastic way, "Sara, welcome to the world of benign fasciculation syndrome."

Benign fasciculation syndrome can be diagnosable but not degenerative in nature or a freak occurrence without explanation. If your arm spasms after lifting weights at the gym, you have experienced the sensation. For a few years, my muscles twitched all around my body, sometimes for hours, just as my dad's had. I wonder now if it was some manifestation of my wigged-out nervous system. I felt the incessant twitching inside my ear. As a band across the back of my head. On my tongue. I once sat through a Sunday service as a large spasm pulsed in my ass. That one? I had to laugh. Then, convinced the spasms were a sign of something worse, I started to pray for healing.

Faith Healing

I found Agnes Sanford's writing in my late thirties and read it with some skepticism, but I was also fascinated by her life. Sanford's healing methods can be pseudoscientific, theologically fringy, and require a disclaimer like "take this with a grain of salt." But there is something pure and clear about how she writes about healing that made me open to her work. In his memoir *Now and Then*, Frederick Buechner talks about attending a few days of prayer seminars led by Sanford, who, he writes,

> was recommended to me by a friend as a fascinating and deeply spiritual woman who had had remarkable success as

> a faith healer. "Spiritual" was another of those words that I always choked on a little, and faith-healing was something I associated with charlatans and the lunatic fringe; but since my friend had only recently left the college chaplaincy to become a Jungian analyst, I couldn't dismiss him as easily taken in, so I decided to accept his recommendation and go.[2]

Buechner was struck by how Sanford began the seminar, not by focusing on healing the body but by first healing the memory. "For God, all time is one, and we were to invite Jesus into our past as into a house that has been locked up for years—to open windows and doors for us so that light and life could enter at last," Buechner says, "to sweep out the debris of decades, to drive back the shadows. The healing of memories was like the forgiveness of sins, she said."[3] The process reminds me of a line from a Catholic deliverance prayer: "Heal the pain of my memories, so that nothing that has happened to me will cause me to remain in pain and anguish, filled with anxiety."[4] The invitation to pray through "locked up" memories was new to me, and I wondered if some stuck anxiety could be loosened by partnering therapeutic work exploring my past with prayer for it.

Sanford died in 1982 in California at age eighty-four. I was four that year, living across the country in an Indiana rancher. Years later, when I read her book, I was used to looking to the past for nostalgia. For comfort, I still cook red sauce classics I ate as a kid: meatball subs and pork parm. I play '80s music on our little portable radio and think of my mom, aunt, and cousin sunbathing on the concrete-slabbed back patio behind our house. Baby oil next to a beach towel, WMEE playing "Jesse's Girl" and "Time After Time," half a watermelon and a single spoon. But I had not ever looked to the past for healing.

The stories of physical healing Sanford tells may not be nostalgic, but they are comforting and devourable. She helps restore the leg of a boy named Sammy by telling him to pray to God, "Look here, I'm boss inside of me and what I say goes. Now get busy and mend that leg."[5] When Sanford lays her hands on the knee of another child, Sally, diagnosed with "infant paralysis," Sally cries, "Oh, take your hands away! . . . It's hot!"[6] There is always heat with my favorite accounts of healing. Like the disciples, Sanford healed with an electric spirit, whether the sick person was a Christian or not. Sanford typically didn't direct the kids she healed to pray to Jesus. Often, the faith conversion came after the miracle.

Healing like Fire

In his 1970 book *Nine O'Clock in the Morning*, Episcopal priest Dennis Bennett writes about how he was as surprised as the rest of his congregation when he received the gift of tongues in the 1960s. Healing followed.

My favorite passage is theatrical. A man named Rupe had lost the use of his diaphragm in a bad accident. One day, Rupe was at a prayer meeting with other members from Bennett's church, including a man named Bill. Rupe shared an account of what happened:

> Suddenly Bill said, "My hands are on fire! They're hurting me!" I said, "Put 'em on me!" I shuffled around the hassock

> on my knees to where Bill and his wife were kneeling, and he laid his hands on my chest. I felt as though all my insides had fallen out! I sprang to my feet, and literally had to grab at my trousers to keep them from falling off; they were suddenly too loose. I had to struggle to get my coat unbuttoned, it was now so tight. The whole outward configuration of my body was changing as my internal organs were renewed and went back into their proper positions. My heart was thumping like a hammer, of course, and I felt it move three or four inches, back into its normal place under my breast-bone. Not only was my diaphragm restored, but my physical body was changed so much that I had to get all new suits![7]

When Sanford talks about healing, it is like a charged battery. She tells the child Sally that God's healing her knee is like "electricity working in your lamp. I guess it has to be hot, so as to make the knee come back to life."[8] Bill's hands were on fire.

This is the way I want to be healed. *God, I want to feel my broken heart move three or four inches to its rightful place.* I want the vibrating I feel in my body to be from the Holy Spirit restoring it, not my nervous system wigging out. I want to be healed from anxiety and the way it physically manifests in my body.

"Nerves are like children," Sanford says.

> They respond to suggestion better than to command. In fact, the subconscious mind that controls the forces of the body has an almost wanton disregard for command. "Relax!" we tell ourselves sternly, and the nerves laugh at us and tighten up more than ever. "Now you're relaxing," we congratulate them, and with a pleased smile they relax. So, we speak gently

> and soothingly to the nerves all the way up the body and in the head.[9]

This description appealed to me. And yet after reading her book, I could not be self-soothed or relaxed. Instead of being healed as a result of my increasingly desperate prayers, my symptoms increased. Some nights, my whole body hummed. *Did I have a seizure? Did I have a stroke? Is it MS or Huntington's?* The volume knob of my anxiety broke off the radio on those nights. Eventually, the morning always came, usually gray. Back to my routine. The weary drag out of bed. Pour the cereal. Put one heel in the foot of my kid's sock, then the other. The backpack, bus, and work. This season of life, when I first experienced benign fasciculation syndrome, is when I learned that the term "emotional hangover" is not a punch line but an actual way of being. I got to know the feeling well: the ache of the limbs, the headache in the back of the eyes.

In the worst months of trembling, I wondered if the cause was mental and not physical at all. I did all the cognitive behavioral therapy exercises I'd been told to try. "Notice the feeling, like a paper boat floating down a river," Sara said to me once in a session. "Let the worry about the feeling pass. Say, 'Hello, feeling.' Breathe." We would practice together over a Zoom screen. If you are anxious before bed, read a little bit. Don't deny the worry; make it a friend. Instead of avoiding anxiety, approach it by exposure to make it smaller. Anxiety is our guest. In some way, hearing her believe that these practices helped made them help. But the problem of my anxiety was chronic. No matter how much relief I felt in the moment, I could not breathe backward and erase the time I'd lost to worry.

Newlywed

My first prolonged season of health anxiety had come years before, arriving in my midtwenties in the fall after I was married. Months after the wedding, in what should have been a sweet time, I became convinced that Drew had cancer because of a palpable lymph node in his neck. My own body anxiety transferred to him in these weeks. He was learning to roast coffee at work and would come home with green coffee beans in his pockets. I used to take a coffee bean I kept on a windowsill in the living room and put it next to the lymph node on his neck to measure it. Smaller than an olive was safe, the medical website said.

One day, I found a dried kidney bean in the pantry and held it next to his neck. The size matched his palpable lymph node. Was a kidney bean smaller than an olive? He rolled his eyes and eventually went to an internist for an exam to appease me. It turns out that my poking at his lymph node had made it tender. As soon as I moved on to the next worry, it shrunk.

Sometimes, to try to understand anxiety, I imagine it has form, like a kidney bean or an olive. I can practically feel anxiety like a smooth stone flanked to my side. Other times, I picture anxiety inside my body. I imagine that processing anxiety is the purpose of an organ we thought was there for no good reason. Maybe, all along, the appendix is where anxiety lives. Anxiety, then, would be about four inches in size and the shape of a small cucumber.

It turns out that I may not be that far off in my imaginings. Recent research findings indicate that anxiety may, in fact, live in the body in more ways than one.

Epigenetics and Generational Trauma

Epigenetics is an emerging research area "that shows how environmental influences—children's experiences—actually affect the expression of their genes." Researchers have documented evidence that anxiety carries generationally in animals. In one experiment, "mice were taught to fear the smell of cherries when the scent was paired with an electric shock. Their mouse children and grandchildren also showed signs of anxiety when exposed to the cherry smell, even though they had never 'learned' the painful association."[10] As I searched for possible root causes of my anxiety that deepened as it grew into young adulthood, I wanted to take a closer look at epigenetics and how it may connect to my Jewish family of origin. How might the environments or experiences of our past affect current generations?

Trauma clearly plays a role in some Jewish people's experience of anxiety. A *Scientific American* article highlights the work of a Jewish researcher on the generational effects of Holocaust descendants. The results of a 2015 study showed "that descendants of people who survived the Holocaust have different stress hormone profiles than their peers, perhaps predisposing them to anxiety disorders."[11]

"Jewish anxiety" may, in fact, be a cultural trope, but it's not something to take lightly. Madison Margolin makes this case in her article "Why Jewish Anxiety Is No Laughing Matter," published in *Forward*. "Woody Allen and Larry David weren't the first ones" among the Jewish people to experience anxiety, Margolin writes. "The book of Genesis defines the people of Israel as 'those who wrestle constantly with G-d and with people.'"[12]

Reading this, I wondered if there is a faint pencil line from the trauma of Jews being expelled from Egypt, from let-my-people-go to the exile of Babylon, the great Jewish diasporas of the past thousands of years, all the persecution, to the Holocaust, to my grandmother, to my father, to me. My born-in-the-1970s body, threaded into a seam of anxious Jewish bodies from the past and into the future.

Seeking Relief

After reading about epigenetics and finding some solidarity but little relief, I tried out other more practical ways to feel less anxious. One New Year's Day, I started to feed myself soft things, launching a month of wellness intended to help me start the new year better than I'd left the old one. I learned that congee, which had seemed impossibly complex to prepare, is simple: sushi rice boiled in a savory broth for hours. I tried "Dryuary," omitting alcohol for a couple of weeks in January, to see if some interior drag would dissipate. I didn't feel any different.

In another attempt at self-care to soothe anxiety, I drove to the co-op and stood in front of the cold case with juices and alternative sugar sodas for several minutes, looking for the most potent combination of ginger and turmeric. I drank nothing but turmeric tea for a week. I imagined my liver soaked in turmeric, floating in a bath of it. I pictured our county coroner wearing a bow tie and a fresh apron, rubber gloves to his elbows, writing in his report, if I were to die, "The liver of a forty-five-year-old woman was an altered hue." The coroner's report is rarely poetic, but in this case, there is a ring to "altered hue." Cut me open and there would be a rush of blood and marigold-colored juice. The apron is streaked gold.

Slowly, I began to understand that my anxiety was not really about my body. It is a way I try to manage uncertainty. Perhaps you do too. Your temporarily able or dis-abled body, whatever state it is in, is a reminder of your uncertain future. Anxiety is also a natural thing. It is a common trait we share. The problem is when the balance gets out of whack and worry becomes monster-size. We do not know if or when a single cell in our body will split and multiply until there is something we can feel under our skin. The pea under the pile of mattresses that causes the whole stack of beds to tumble.

But when it is proportionate with other parts of your life, anxiety can just be a part of you, and there is a flip side. Maybe, like me, you would not be as imaginative if you were not also anxious. Or you would not be as sharp, intuitive, or an excellent judge of character without the tentativeness that comes from being anxious. Or you would not be a researcher and methodical if you did not first learn how to turn over all causes, possible reasons, and outcomes. Looking at it this way, we see that anxiety is not necessarily our enemy, an understanding that can bring us some consolation.

I also experienced relief of a different kind. One day, after visits to a neurologist and other specialists for tests to rule out degenerative muscle diseases that may have been causing my muscle spasms, I was told I am not, indeed, diagnosable. The cause of my symptoms is, in fact, benign. And then one day, as quickly as the trembling came, with little explanation or fanfare, it stopped three years after it began.

Once the physical symptoms dissipated and I was no longer focused on physical healing, I began to experience something new: a gentle tug toward an even broader expression of what it means to get well. In the body, yes, but also in the spirit.

3

Path of Wellness

A few years later, a friend sent me an article about an "all-inclusive wellness retreat" in the Catskill Mountains in *T Magazine*. "The name Hemlock Neversink might conjure a wooded fairyland, and that idea isn't too far from the truth."[1] You can bird-watch and try something called "pine needle weaving." You can experience animal therapy with the retreat center's goats. In the website's trailer, cute goats slo-mo leap across a stony brook. "Their calm demeanor, even when chewing their cud, can inspire a meditative state that's relaxing to be around. Because goats are calm and in the present moment, humans can't help but take on that energy. Life's stresses simply melt away."[2]

The guesthouse is shown in golden sunset light. "The property's design draws from the region's Quaker heritage, with a neutral color palette, ash and walnut furniture, and quilt-inspired custom wool rugs."[3] There is a close-up of a masseuse's thumb running over a guest's left eyebrow.

Upon arrival, guests are asked to complete a survey to customize their stay: "How structured do you like your days?" and "Would you like to move or rest?"[4]

If they asked *me* how I would like to move or rest, I would tell them this: I would like to rest with Jesus in a grassy field from the 1970s in the Catskill Mountains, a holy retreat. I would like to sleep on Jesus's stomach with a lamb's wool laid over his lap. In prayer in the past month, I imagined these scenes. They kept coming. I would like to sit with the resurrected Jesus on a log around a beach fire and eat grilled fish.

Years ago, when my friend Meg turned forty, she took a trip to Tulum, Mexico, with her sister-in-law and best friend. They surprised Meg with a session where she was carried into the water by a yogi or some sort of spiritual guide, and for an hour she was swayed back and forth in his arms in the ocean, in loops and dips, like a baby. She later said she let some things go in that hour. She trusted him, cried, and released things that you can see clearly enough at forty to release.

I, too, would like to move or rest cradled like a baby, to be held by Jesus in the sea. I close my eyes and picture it: Jesus is waist-deep in a white robe. I am dead limp, with no irony or embarrassment. No male gaze or body judgment. No workweek professionalism or makeup. My own body, as she is, with more than an inch of skin to grab. With asymmetry and cellulite. With dead skin and dandruff. Always dry. The real self, in real arms.

In my imagination, I am not sure if the arms of Jesus are resurrected, and in my imagination, I do not check for stigmata. I do not think about whether I am back in Bible times or the present day. I am simply in the water, falling back, heaving forward. Around me: strips of bulbous seaweed—ribbon kelp, mermaid's bladder, and sea otter's cabbage—moving in and out with the tides.

Peace for Sale

Some of the things I can buy to help my body and soul? I can't make them up. In the same article that features Hemlock Neversink, I read about the recently launched High Light Rituals, a line of "dainty necklaces and bracelets that are handmade in New York and Rhode Island."[5]

For $115, I can buy a silk bracelet with instructions for a ritual to cast love spells. I can add to my online shopping cart necklaces that "feature gemstones including citrine (which High Light says is 'a stone of abundance'), labradorite (meant to channel intuition) and Herkimer diamonds (to amplify spiritual awareness)." I can also order an altar kit containing "a ritual designed to cleanse and shield." The nineteen-piece set is used to "clear away energetic debris, experience peace and access divine protection," including crystals: "Smoky and Lemurian Quartz, Hematite and Black Tourmaline." As the ceremony concludes, I read that I will find myself "harmonizing with the universe's rhythm, [my] energy purified and safeguarded, and glowing with divine light."[6]

I do not order the silk spell bracelet, gemstone necklace, or altar kit. Maybe if I did, I would be more embodied and my anxiety would lower, but I can't get over the flowery language written for someone younger. Someone who knows the genus of the plants in their house and probably gives each ficus a human name.

My own ceremony kit of gathered objects, or the closest I have to one, contains four unremarkable pieces: a red blanket imported from India I found at a store on Vashon Island, a taper candle in a finger loop holder, a book of Three Stars safety matches, and a cup of coffee. In the early morning, my ritual is to sit and read something from Saint Ignatius, then an epistle, a psalm, or something from the prophets. Here, my anxiety is at its lowest. I sit in the dark sunroom and do the Ignatian Exercises, pacing my way through the nine-month retreat. I wonder, Would my ritual look as ridiculous to some people as the altar kit sounds to me, a nonbeliever in the power of crystals and spells?

Running from Aging

Now that I'm in my midforties, my skin routine has a ritual, and it is much more in line with products featured in the *T Magazine* article. In the morning, hydroiodic acid to hydrate and reduce fine lines and vitamin C serum to brighten. In the evening, lactic acid to exfoliate or retinol to boost collagen production. I apply sunscreen in the morning and afternoon. I wear a baseball hat and sunglasses outside. I wear neck hankies and turtlenecks. I take vitamin D supplements to account for the lost sun exposure. I wake up with new wrinkles and puffy eyes anyway. A serum may slow the effects of aging, but nothing you put on your skin can undo the toll taken by life and by the stressors that accelerate it.

I'm not the only one who is visibly aging. One pastor friend posted on social media photos of himself taken before and after the pandemic. His forehead was baby-ass smooth before the pandemic but had strong, deep lines three years later. His hair is now mostly gray.

We all age—sometimes faster than at other times. The question is, Do we resist?

"I don't want to look like a clown," I've heard people who are considering a cosmetic procedure say. "Just the best version of myself." The offenses of maturation spots on the cheeks, visible pores, and broken blood vessels are answered—by those who can afford treatments—with lasers, microdermabrasion, and derma-blading. Or with Botox, fillers, and other injectables. Scripture tells us, "Do not store up for yourselves treasures on earth, where moth and rust consume and where thieves break in and steal; but store up for yourselves treasures in heaven, where neither moth nor rust consumes and where thieves do not break in and steal. For where your treasure is, there your heart will be also" (Matt. 6:19–21 NRSV). If I judge anyone else for considering these procedures, it's no more than I judge myself for focusing on the treasure on earth that is the skin. A face treasure. A treasure trove of skin smoothies and serums. Skin gyms, skin cycling.

Slap the cheeks and forehead to wake up collagen, but gently. Stretch the skin, and make weird jaw faces to firm the jowl. Ice under the eyes in the morning and a lip mask at night. Sleep on the back to promote healthy lymphatic flow.

The desire for a perfect face and body is a disordered and anxious longing, one that's rooted in ageism, capitalism, and the fear of change. Both women and men learn how older women are to be treated based on what we observe. Society still messages that when we reach a certain age, usually forty, or fifty if we're lucky, women are less valuable. That we are more devalued after we bear children, if able, and further diminished after we can no longer work or produce.

Amid these forces, we experience a deeper craving for relief from the anxiety of aging. This craving, however, is not physical in nature but spiritual. The desire, the true matter of longing, is to be made new. Along with wanting to be wantable, we feel a base desire to be made whole. The desire for youth is a longing for restoration.

Good Enough to Eat

Beauty culture critic Jessica DeFino reported on "the rise and rise of 'dewy dumpling skin'" after noticing "a glut of recent beauty trends that promise to make you look less like you and more like a variety of foodstuffs: . . . glazed donut skin, blueberry milk nails . . ."[7]

DeFino highlights a couple of root causes underlying this edible skin trend. The first is consumerism, because "beauty has become synonymous with buying. After all, when you see glazed doughnut skin it's not skin you're seeing, it's the layer of sheer, shiny, mass-produced skincare formulas on top of it."[8] The second is dehumanization, which "is always on the menu when it comes to female beauty standards. Throughout history women were peaches, pieces of meat, their skin compared to porcelain—a plate on which their beauty (cheeks like apples, lips like cherries) was served. Today, skin is the main course. Skincare commands a larger portion of the beauty market pie than make-up and haircare combined."[9] This is true to my experience. I may not buy a lot of accessories of the purse or earring variety, but if I have a few extra dollars at the end of the month, I will likely spend it on a new serum.

The market is happy to serve up an army of treatments waiting to rejuvenate my middle-aged skin. And the messages about remaining supple and buoyant contrast hard in my mind with the current state of my aging parents. Anyone in the sandwich generation is low-hanging fruit for someone selling a session at a med spa cloaked as a self-care day. At least I am.

In addition to my mother's skin, I've noticed her hands changing over the last many years. As a kid, I would look at my Italian grandmother's arthritic hands; they were already blue-veined and thin-skinned. Once at dinner when I was in my twenties, my Jewish grandmother, Roz, looked at my hands. "You have young hands," she said. I wanted it to feel important since I rarely saw Roz and was disconnected from her geographically and emotionally. I tried but could not find meaning in what she said. Decades later, I can see that the comment was more about her than me. A reflection on how she had once been in my seat across the table.

I put retinol and sunblock on my hands now. My skin is thinner, the sunspots emerging. Stack my daughter's hands, my hands, and my mother's hands in a pile, and it's easy to see: Youth, of course, is a vantage point.

A New Body

I want a new body for my father, who is hunched, shrunken, radiated, scanned, chemo-ed, and biopsied. I want a new body for my mother, who is skin and bones, flared up, and for hours of the day achy like a dull fire.

My wanting a brand-new body, something so fresh it may be described as edible, is a direct response to seeing the age-devoured bodies of my parents. What I feel is not as simple as denial. It is a need for concrete, God-given proof that we will all one day receive bodies like suits of light.

Back when I held the capital youth offered, I would not let myself be desirable. If I had known in my twenties how quickly youth would pass, would I have made different choices about how I moved through the world that would cause me to feel differently about my body today?

Perhaps. Perhaps not. And really, I did know a lot of things about myself in my twenties. I resisted leveraging my body then because I knew it could lead to craving more instead of being satisfied. In its worst distortion, maybe the power I would have gained through spending the capital youth offered could have backfired, turning me into a crone craving a magic mirror to return the power once I'd lost it.

I pay attention to wisdom from people with different journeys into aging who move beyond wellness culture. Women like Anne Lamott, who write honestly about not just aging's difficulties but also its gifts, such as "the precipitous decline in melodrama. Enjoying how unremarkable life is takes practice and time, and then the little things start to shine and delight. . . . Life gets smaller and in its smallness it starts winking at you."[10] I've seen the beginning of life shrinking and am starting to notice how a healthy limiting of options can lower anxiety.

Like Anne, I want to be less dramatic, and I am fine with feeling small. The problem with that scale is the imagination. Flirting with wellness culture can be a form of escapism, even if you are a wellness lurker like me. Instead of visiting Hemlock Neversink, which I cannot afford, I find sarcastic bits of website copy about goats, look at photos of the beautiful grounds, and read reviews.

In my regular life, which is extraordinarily privileged but still runs anxious, I don't need pine needle weaving, an altar kit, or another vitamin C serum. These things are not bad; they are not immoral. But the question, How would I like to move and rest? That is important. And the answer is simple: as a less anxious person who practices self-care not out of comparison, compulsion, or avoidance but because it models a sabbath posture.

I imagine this kind of world: Where rest is not a luxury, synonymous with distraction or equated with boredom. Where rest is not a marker of status when presented as leisure or out of reach for the overworked, burned-out, or always on-call. I would only like this rest if my neighbor, too, can find it. It's not something we can earn or qualify for by being good. The kind of rest I'm looking for? I wonder if it is something we can discover through care.

4

Sundowning

I woke up to nineteen missed calls from Dad. The first text message had come at 2:00 a.m. I did not see them until I woke up at 7:00:

> Help us At emergency room tootem lake hospital. Mom had a total breakdown. Probably from increase in drugs. Evergreen hospital

Then, at 2:07:

> Not good at all seeing monster convinced I am killing her. What the heck

> Where r u

> Big time priblm

I jerked out of bed and called him. I waited, desperate for him to answer. The sun was up. I could see it shining through the blinds, casting its light on the wall opposite my bed.

"We're at the hospital," Dad said. "Mom was seeing devils and demons in the living room last night. People who had been long gone came to life in her head. She was screaming . . . wailing. How did the neighbors not knock on the door," he wondered—to himself as much as to me. They must have been convinced he was strangling her.

There is a word for early evening disorientation experienced by some people with dementia. It's called "sundowning." It reminds me of "sunsetting," a word I recently heard used at work as a euphemism for firing an ad agency. We soon learned from the medical staff that Dad had been correct. Mom had been diagnosed with Parkinson's several years before, and an increase in one of her meds had caused her to weave in and out of confusion, delirium, and full-blown psychosis, which spiked in the nighttime.

Now by her hospital bed, I listened as Mom, mildly sedated, tried to recount what happened the night before. She was unsure if she had dreamed it or had walked through the door and seen someone sitting on the bed in their apartment. "It was a *mhneee*."

"What Mom? I didn't understand you."

"You know, one of those thin guys—thin and tall," she said. "They paint their faces white."

"Oh, a *mime*. That must have been scary, Mom."

During a session with my therapist the next week, Sara dispelled the idea that what Mom said about me in those days were true confessions finally emerging from her deep subconscious. Such as when Mom, that first night at the hospital, spat out that I never loved her. Sara explained that it did not mean deep down she believed she was not loved by me but that in psychosis the mind floats to all iterations of reality and is often far from fact. It still stung.

I kept notes when Mom was in the hospital. I kept notes to keep control. I took the posture of journalist, record keeper, and armchair genealogist. It helps to have a self-assigned job to do when your mother is delirious. The person who carried me in her body was fully out of her mind. It was my notes that held me together.

Music helped. Driving to and from the hospital, I would try to process what I'd seen. I could only listen to people who had pain in their voices: Tom Waits, Sharon Jones, Greg Brown, Charles Bradley, Lucinda Williams. Before, when I'd heard their voices, I'd felt like an inexperienced kid. Now, driving on the 405, they were my peers.

My Mother's Body

In a scene from the 1990s movie version of *Little Women*, Susan Sarandon, playing the family matriarch, Marmee, works scarlet fever out of her daughter Beth's feet. She tells her daughter Jo to get a basin of water, vinegar, and rags. "We must draw the fever out from her head," she says, rubbing Beth's legs and feet until her fever breaks in the morning. In the next scene, Beth is shown sitting up next to the bed, looking well, eating a spoonful of porridge.[1]

I thought of the scene as I sat in the hospital and rubbed Mom's feet, frozen from Parkinson's. Mom could not sit up and would not get better. I put red socks with grippy hearts on her feet. Leftovers in a hospital sock bin from Valentine's Day. Even then, just four months earlier, she had smiled and eaten a Black Forest cupcake at our family table. Now, she weighed eighty-four pounds. I could lift her, like my eleven-year-old daughter.

I rubbed and rubbed her feet in the cherry-red hospital socks with stickies on the soles shaped like hearts. Her heart beat and blood circulated in her limbs, but she could not move with ease. Later that evening, I held her legs open while the nurse inserted a catheter.

I have an early memory of sitting between my mother's legs on the shag carpet while she peeled kernel shells out of each piece of popcorn before putting it in my hands. Her legs formed a *V* shape to keep me close, a natural boundary.

In the hospital room, I put my hands on her head and prayed that she would be healed. Only part of me believed it could happen, but all of me wanted it to.

As a child, I would lie next to her in her bed while she moved her hands through my hair, cascading strands through her fingers. She was always there in her hands. We were still and safe between her pink, flannel sheets in the big bed with the mauve comforter, my head touched with the same careful hands that peeled away popcorn kernel skins. Now, her hands were shaking, frozen.

Unprepared

In hospitals, time is droopy. It bends and stretches; the clock hands are like putty. It is surreal, like the Dalí painting, *The Persistence of Memory*. The hospital light is white, restless.

"We didn't expect this one," Dad said as I walked him through sterile, bright hallways to the car after Mom's first night in the hospital. I'd arrived at the ER with a bag packed for an overnight and encouraged him to go home and rest.

I tried to comfort him. I explained how Mom was safe and calm from the Valium she'd been given. She would sleep and so should he. I wish I had been born with a more natural inclination to caregiving. I wish I was not a person who carries anxiety in my thighs and stomach—a worry baby. Sciatica caused not by a true pregnancy but by a ghost infant of worry.

A lifetime of false health alarms and precatastrophizing phantom symptoms had left Dad surprisingly calm in the aftermath of an actual emergency. There is no hierarchy of intensity in his brain. Anxiety about the body is so woven into his thinking that a small thing, a blood bruise, is as concerning as his blood cancer. The worst has already happened, and he is still anticipating what is next. The worry extends to all possible conditions and maladies.

The next morning, Mom was moved to a shared room with three other patients. The dry-erase board told me the date, Father's Day. It also recorded the other patients' first names. Barb to Mom's right. She has Parkinson's too and kept mumbling, "Daisy. Help me. Help me, Daisy." She is alone. There is no Daisy in the room or on the board.

Lavonna is by the window getting an eye exam. Her son calls and she puts him on speaker. He says it's 100 degrees in Arizona. "I love you, Mom," he tells her. "If you get bored, you can always call me."

I am totally jealous. I dislike myself for the feeling, but I want to sip an Arnold Palmer and golf in sweltering Phoenix. I want all this to just be a phone call from some other place. I want my hair to blow in the wind as the golf cart whizzes to the back nine. I want a Father's Day corn-on-the-cob-and-deviled-egg picnic. I want to rip cold shrimp from the tail and sip a colder martini. I do not want to be here by the beeping monitor, the kidney bean–shaped puke tray, and the motorized bed. It's the way her mouth looks, sleeping, mostly open.

The fourth hospital roommate is Francis. He has not eaten in a day. His daughter-in-law visits. Very pretty, she holds up a bite of mac and cheese. "Flynn," as she calls him, "it's Cassie. I'm not going to feed you; I'm just going to hold this spoon next to your nose. *Mmmmm*. Doesn't this smell good?" The pretty daughter-in-law had to leave because Flynn pooped in the bed, and a nurse had to roll in a privacy screen and clean him up. "Happy Father's Day, Flynn, hope you can watch the Mariners game!" Cassie calls, backing out the door. And with that, she is gone.

Daisy, it turns out, is not imagined but a very real fifty-something daughter who arrived at our shared room with a confidence that shows she's done this care thing before. She asks Barb the right questions: Do you want a warm blanket? Can I get you something to drink, Mom, like tea? I can only compare her easy competence to my fumblings, unsure how to maneuver the hospital bed and forgetting to hold Mom's robe closed when she shuffles to the bathroom. Her crepey skin hangs like dollops of frosting off two bony spoons, on full display for Flynn. Mom would be embarrassed, but she is not.

The better, wiser Daisy would have known to hold the robe closed as her mother walked to the bathroom. She brought flowers and wanted to show Barb the view from a nearby window. "I'd like to take you in a wheelchair so you can see the outside world a little bit, Mom. Is it OK if I open the curtain so you can see the view from here?"

As Daisy sweeps the drape open, she bumps over the vase of flowers she brought. Water pours onto the floor, and glass shatters into pieces. "I'm a bad person," Daisy tells a nurse who comes to help. "I made a mess. I'm sorry, Mom."

No one knows how to do this.

Blue Nights

Joan Didion writes about "blue nights," the time around the summer solstice of long twilights when blue sky stays bright even in the dark, in her memoir of the same name. Any remaining sunlight is a different shade of blue.

Didion sat in hospital rooms as a caregiver and patient. She knew double grief, losing her husband, John Dunne, and daughter, Quintana Roo, within eighteen months. "This book is called 'Blue Nights' because at the time I began it I found my mind turning increasingly to illness, to the end of the promise, the dwindling of the days, the inevitability of the fading, the dying of the brightness," Didion explains.[2] Grief-avoidant, I was not ready to read *Blue Nights* when it was published in 2011. When Mom was in the hospital more than a decade later, I devoured it. To calm my anxiety by remembering the universal nature of suffering, I looked for someone who had survived and recorded an account of a much worse turn.

Didion didn't experience blue nights living in LA, but she did in New York. I spent two summers in New York under an orange sky, everything in an electric fog. Maybe you could see a star. Cross the bridge, get out to Nyack, and gulp in the air. You don't know what you're in until you're out.

In the spring, we wait for the sky to stay light longer. "Look," I'll tell my son and daughter when we reach April. "You can see the mountains until 8:00 p.m." Our view from the couch: a stretch of the Cascades, a little darker than the sky up top. Soon the peaks will be visible until 8:30 p.m. By late July we forget to look. In the Northwest, we'll have light till after 10:00 p.m. at solstice.

Summer solstice is tomorrow at 7:57 a.m. The year split in half, moving toward the light and away from it. I, too, am moving forward while my mother's life falls back.

I pray, *We'll take a little light, please, God. We'll take it for a little longer.*

Fear of Falling

Mom was diagnosed with Parkinson's in the summer of 2016. The disease is incurable; patients progressively lose dopamine until symptoms like tremors increase and gait noticeably diminishes. For several years, it progressed slowly. When Michael J. Fox was diagnosed with early onset Parkinson's in his twenties, a doctor told him he would have maybe ten good years before the disease really progressed. In the years after Mom's diagnosis, I anxiously monitored for precursors in Parkinson's patients diagnosed young, small signs that it could be in me too.

Often, Mom said if a doctor hadn't diagnosed her, she would not have believed she had the disease. In those first years, to meet her would have been like meeting anyone else. She worked at a Seattle-based health clinic as a patient services representative. She bought citrus at Whole Foods. She talked for hours on the phone with her sister back in Indiana.

Some days it never came to her mind. Other days, maybe her thumb twitched. My thumb would twitch. Maybe she woke up in a scream, a nightmare where she was being chased. A little bloody murder. I wondered if I had those kinds of audible nightmares too.

Anytime Drew said he slept badly, I asked him if I had been restless or vocal in sleep. I couldn't feel my own twitches, eye flutters, or sore legs and not think about my mother. I am vigilant. I monitor and watch. You can't get a thing past me.

Now we lose more and more of her at a noticeable clip. The clock is warped, but the hands are still circling. As dopamine evaporates in her brain, we move into a midwinter pace of decline. A minute a day of cognition, maybe two. For a long time, you couldn't detect the change in her thinking. For a long time, even I, who'd appropriated the symptoms of her real disease onto my imaginary diagnosis, did not notice her slow decline.

But there came a moment, a time on some clock somewhere unmarked, when her condition had progressed to the point that I had no choice but to accept that she was not going to get better. I could worry about any sign of my own theoretical diagnosis as a disordered distraction, but there was no longer anything theoretical about hers.

She is skin stretched over bones. You can see her entire rib cage, everything. I see her pelvis, hip bone, and shoulder blade.

In *Blue Nights*, Didion, who later was also diagnosed with Parkinson's, talks about her fear of falling, her frailty. My mother's skeleton is there, covered by flesh, but she is brittle. Every day, I worry about her falling.

Recently, I listened to a writer I admire talk about her career and how stopping work to take care of her aging parents would have held her back. So she opted out. She let them navigate illness on their own.

I had never heard anyone speak about their parents in that way before. The writer was not just expressing avoidant behavior; I have plenty of that myself and can relate. But this writer was making a bold declaration by refusing to care for her family. She put the life preserver on herself, and herself alone, before anyone else, and if she felt guilt about that, she did not express it. "Of course, I'd put the mask on a kid first if the plane is going down," most of us say. I wondered what it would say about me if I made the choice to stop caregiving. I know the higher calling of caregiving: Accept pain, ambiguity, and long-suffering. In my heart's heart, at times I want to opt out. Here is where I need Jesus to form me. Through caregiving, I understand more of my lack.

Formed by Love

It would be horrible to lose any member of my family. I can imagine it, even though I would never choose it. What I can't do is imagine myself without writing. I wondered what that meant. In *Monsters*, Claire Dederer asks the question, Would I be a better mother if I wasn't a writer? And more potently, Would I be a better writer if I was not a mother?[3] If my not being able to imagine no longer writing was evidence of profound selfishness and indulgent fantasy that did not involve family, then I'd write alone, and I'd die alone on a little raised bed with a dog by my side. Like the old man, also a writer, at the start of Sherwood Anderson's *Winesburg, Ohio.*

> The idea had got into his mind that he would some time die unexpectedly and always when he got into bed he thought

> of that. It did not alarm him. The effect, in fact, was quite a special thing and not easily explained. It made him more alive, there in the bed, than at any other time. Perfectly still he lay and his body was old and not of much use any more, than at any other time. He was like a pregnant woman, only that thing inside him was not a baby but a youth.[4]

The writer in the story goes on to dream on his raised bed about a series of people who, because of being exposed to the truth, become grotesque. But not the writer. "It was the young thing inside him that saved the old man."[5] I believe that the young thing inside me, and you, is timeless. It's our Creator, God, who makes seeds sprout, kids grow into teenagers with awkward, sprawly limbs, and dogs sigh when they nap in a way that makes you love them completely.

In a 2009 PBS interview, Kathleen Norris talked about her book *Acedia and Me*. Norris had been prolific for decades but paused writing for a time. After seven years, she published *Acedia and Me*. "In some senses this book is a miracle to me because I was able to finish it at all," she said.[6]

In the pause, Norris became a full-time caregiver for her husband, father, sister, and mother. "All thought of writing was . . . shoved to the side for me," she said.

> One of the reasons I decided that I'd better not have children is because I really didn't want to be a caregiver. So it is something that has been imposed on me, and I have really had to learn how to cope with that, how to be patient and loving instead of irritable and impatient and, believe me, it is a struggle, and I don't always make it. To think, if I'm with this person, helping them do this ordinary task, like going to the bathroom, that's the most important thing I can be

> doing with my life at the moment—to convince myself of that every day.[7]

Fully submitting your calling, vocation, and time to caring for other people is incredibly ordinary and hidden work. There is no fame or accolades in this kind of labor.

Norris moved past the mundane to be better formed. Compelled by love for another, she seems to have moved closer to God. I'd argue this is holy work. Caregiving is like praying, in a closet, with the door closed. No one is looking, and if they could look, there wouldn't be much to see. This is inner work, and I am at the beginning. I am anxious about whether I am qualified to be a caregiver, especially in the moment while I am trying to care. I am still kicking and screaming into this work. Rubbing the feet in the red heart socks brings out my "irritable and impatient" nature.

Grow Up

Maybe, like me, you are full of recriminations. Grow up, you want to tell yourself. You benefited from the care of your parents in a million ways, and putting them first is the least you can do. It's how Jesus would act if he was in your place. But you wonder, Wouldn't Jesus rather be sanding a table or roasting fish on a fire than feeding a sick family member porridge or helping them get ready for bed? Sure, he was human.

You're a little nicer to yourself then. You stop looking for something transcendent in caregiving, you stop waiting for someone to plop a fat caregiving medal around your neck. In other words, you grow up. You set boundaries. I remembered what my friend Tony said when Dad got sick: "You can never do enough. There will always be more to do, so be boundaried to sustain your energy."

If you can keep at your work even a little, you do it. If you need to stop for a while, maybe you'll enter into a time of "deep spiritual struggle to overcome [your] resistance," like Norris.[8] Gradually, you begin to feel relieved that you are taking care of someone who needs you with no one watching. This is not performative care. When taking care of someone—after the emotional sludge surfaces—there is freedom in more fully knowing yourself and being known by God. Maybe you are more grounded and aware of God's presence in the most ordinary things.

Beauty in Suffering

The memory returns to me again and again: She used to take the popcorn shells out of each kernel. I sat in between her legs, a boundary in *V* formation. Last night in the hospital when Mom was hallucinating, a few minutes before she told me I was trying to kill her, she told me in tears that she loved me from my first kick. She would love me until the end.

We hosted two friends from Indiana when they were visiting Seattle. Robin and Nancy are about the same age as Mom. Walking through the house, they asked about different photographs and objects. We came across a basket of coffee cherries we'd plucked from our coffee tree on the porch and had set to dry on the windowsill. Drew grew the plant from a start, and it's taller than we are now. The three of us sat around the basket in the kitchen, chatting as we peeled back the dried red fruit to reveal the bean. "I love working with women," Nancy said.

I wanted Mom to be there too. When she was younger, Mom worked with her hands. The needlepoint candle ornament we hang on the Christmas tree each December reminds me of my mother's former precision. She was a surgical technician at a hospital when I was a young child, handing instruments to surgeons in the operating room. She drove me around town with sharp and quick reflexes. I knew and loved her in physical and mental health, and I know and love her now when she is limited in mobility and full of confusion.

How Mom cries out to God in moments of psychosis and hallucination messes me up. *Do something, God*, I pray. *Show up. Mom is left to suffer, and this is the sound of it.* Jesus died with a whole mind. It is easier to not worry like the birds and the flowers when you are not terrified.

My friend Beth said that when her mother's mind degenerated, she prayed God would work in her spirit, in a hidden place of the mind that is unseen. A place that the caregiver may or may not ever see. I can see Mom's faith, carrying the wooden cross we brought back from St. Paul's in London inside of her purse. Finding the cross on her pillow. The breath prayer book by the bed.

Still, unexplainable, in the presence of physical wasting and dementia, there is something true and good growing in my mom. Her spirit is suffering, but it is not anxious. Her concern may be disoriented, but it is on the here and now, in getting through the present moment. My anxiety is so theoretical and future-focused. Mom's is about pain that I would do anything to take away. When I was sick as a kid, she told me she wanted to be sick on my behalf. Now a mother, I understand. In the presence of her suffering, there is a beauty that emerges alongside her resilience. The suffering of a person we love is not ours to take away. But we can love them through it.

5

Hotel Corazón

After three days on new meds, Mom was stable enough to be discharged from the hospital. We drove home on summer solstice, past an outdoor mall. Shoppers were eating orange blossom ice cream, walking purebreds, buying lipstick at Sephora.

"I didn't know we were so close to the mall," Mom said.

A couple sat outside eating vegan Thai. Kids walked by drinking bubble tea. Someone was going inside a day spa called Yuan.

At Yuan, clients begin a hydrotherapy circuit with a 100- to 105-degree hot pool to "heat the body and soften the skin." Next, they "submerge in the cool pool"—70 to 85 degrees—that "reoxygenates and replenishes your deep tissues." In the eucalyptus steam room, you can "enjoy the twinkling lights and uplifting aromas" before moving to something called the ice cave. You end in the salt room—155 to 165 degrees—where "Himalayan salt helps to counterbalance the influx of positive ions from the many electronic devices we use every day."[1]

How do I know all this? I spent $59 at Yuan for a one-hour spa pass a couple of weeks later. I tried the hydrotherapy circuit: the hot pool, the cool pool, the steam room, the ice cave, and the salt room. I felt depleted and dehydrated afterward. My limbs were heavy. Maybe that meant it was healing, if healing is supposed to begin by hollowing out.

Home

It is now evening of the day of Mom's discharge, and I am home on the porch. Mom is sleeping in the spare room in our basement for a few nights before returning to her and Dad's apartment, a ten-minute drive from our house. I try to leave her in the guest room in the same way I used to leave my daughter at night when I finally got her down. I lie on my stomach and army crawl out to the door so as not to wake Mom. Now I am quiet in the not-quite-dark, hoping she doesn't wake up. Waking can lead to confusion, delirium, paranoia, and finally mania. A chain of mental events that runs a terrifying loop. Her cry, when it comes, is like a child's.

It is the queen of blue nights. It's dark now. I light a candle on the porch. Camille Saint-Saëns's "Danse Macabre" is playing on the classical station. The host reads a rough translation after the piece ends: "Eat drink and be merry, because no matter your station in life, you're going to end up six feet under. . . . Support for Classical King comes from the Seattle Symphony, performing Mahler's Resurrection Symphony," the ad break.[2]

First, the dog whines to come out, then whines to go in, not noticing she is standing on sugar someone spilled on the terra cotta. If she had stopped to lick it, she would have whined for more. I can make out a crescent moon through a few tall evergreens. Eagles rest on those trees in the daytime; I've seen them. Maybe they do at night, too, in a huge nest with one wing stretched out toward the moon, the other to the Olympics. I look at the moon again, and I wonder what time it is.

As I was helping Mom get ready for bed that evening, in my head, I was in Spain. Beforehand, I had read an article in *The New York Times* about a new boutique hotel—Hotel Corazón in Majorca, off the east coast of Spain near Ibiza—that wants to host my "hot girl summer."[3]

I help my mother change into her night diaper and oversized T-shirt. I hold her shoulder, bony, and see her ribs, protruding, while she feels for the bathroom seat. I unwind toilet paper and hand it to her, turning away so she can have some illusion of privacy.

Dad triple-diapered my daughter once before taking her out for the day. Nothing was going to get through. I laughed about it at the time. He also triple-diapered my mother last week while getting her ready for the night. I don't know what is funny or sad anymore.

After reading the article, I visit the Hotel Corazón website, saturated in red with a top-of-the-fold video of naked models prancing on rocks. A perpetual coin toss between another white sangria or another orgasm. The homepage says: "HERE, A NEW WAY OF BEING IS POSSIBLE, RULED BY EASY

LIVING AND EVERYDAY ADVENTURE. YOU CAN'T BREAK THE RULES BECAUSE THERE ARE NONE."

I support Mom as she climbs into bed, navigating the rail we slid between the mattress and box spring.

"HOTEL CORAZÓN IS A HAVEN FOR WILD ALCHEMY. IT'S A MALLORCA LUXURY HOTEL FOR A NEW GENERATION OF TRAVELERS WHO WANT TO BE BAREFOOT, EAT STRAIGHT FROM THE TREES, SWIM IN THE SEA AT NIGHT, AND GET LOST IN THE PINES. IT'S A PLACE TO MEDITATE UNDERWATER AND JUMP ROCKS WITH WILD MOUNTAIN GOATS."

I turn out the light and walk upstairs to clean the living room: MAGNA-TILES, LEGOs, newspaper, toilet paper rolls the dog has shredded. I hear my name and go back downstairs, telling myself to stay calm. Mom is nervous about her pills. Was I sure she took the right dosage before bed? Am I sure the dosage is correct for tomorrow?

"WE BELIEVE FOOD SHOULD BE LOCAL, SEASONAL, MEDICINAL, AND DELICIOUS. FOR THESE REASONS, WE'VE LOVINGLY RETURNED HOTEL CORAZÓN'S LAND TO ITS ORIGINAL PURPOSE—A FERTILE, ABUNDANT FARM."

Upstairs, I begin to sort laundry. Half of my pants are too small. I pour a premixed jalapeño margarita, which I bought on impulse from Target.

"HOTEL CORAZÓN IS A PLACE TO DO THINGS YOU'RE AFRAID OF, OR TO DO SWEET NOTHING. IT'S A PLACE TO LOSE AND FIND YOURSELF AT THE SAME TIME."[4]

We DoorDash subs from Tubs for dinner. I eat an Italian grinder and a bag of potato chips.

Labor

Tonight, during Mom's sundowning, I spent an hour trying things to calm her down. First, her short, curt breaths. The only thing to compare them to is labor. But less "hoo hoo, hee hee" and more like choppy waves—if waves were breath. The lungs doing a sort of staccato.

Next, Mom sits very straight. Sometimes she stands to see if it helps. I took her hands to steady her as she tried to stand. She started shuffling forward while I shuffled backward, a sort of dance. I fanned her arms out and in, like we were playing an imaginary accordion.

In a stretch of time when a person is frozen from Parkinson's, you try to take their mind to less painful places. You become nostalgic by default. "Remember the old house?" You try the senses. "Dad ordered grouper for room service in Florida. Can you still remember the smell?" You move to facts. "What floor were your three apartments located on when you and Dad lived in that building in downtown Fort Wayne? Could you see the river from the living room in all of them?" You fumble around YouTube for a meditation video. You try rain sounds, bird sounds. "Remember the Northern Cardinals in Indiana?" You ask about her favorite bird. They reverse formation at the Rockies, and Mom hasn't seen one in years.

I moved to Seattle first, with Drew. My parents moved over those mountains to join us.

What time is it? How long have I been doing this? I look at my watch.

Imagine yourself here. You are sitting your mother down now because the shuffling and air accordion playing didn't ease her pain. You are rubbing her legs, holding one heel, and moving your knuckles up and down her calf. Not too soft, not too hard. She is grunting, shaking, trying to keep present in the pain. You want to say she is doing this for a reason, that she is working toward a goal, jargon you hear exercise instructors say.

But there is the truth. There is always the truth. This is going to get harder, never better. You want to pray for her to be healed. You think, *It will probably not work, but it could.* It might make you bitter. It might make you question God's goodness. Go ahead and be angry. Ask God why he doesn't show up, realize God is showing up through your care. You feel like that is not nearly enough, and yet it is somehow abundant.

You look up; she is calmer. She is tired, her eyes fluttering and half closed. You walk her down the stairs, counting down twelve steps with her to the ground floor. "Good job. One more step. OK. Let's pee." A new diaper, pink with a flower on the front. The oversized T-shirt. A wet rag for her face, then lotion. "Do you want to brush your teeth?"

You get her in bed, float the comforter over her body, and situate the pillow. You remember Dad is in the living room waiting to be walked to his car. You run back upstairs and help him down the front porch steps so he can drive home and sleep in his own bed. The railing is wound with wisteria the former owners of the house grew. As he shuffles down, leaves fling in his face. It smells like sweet peas. He twists his hands around stems to find the thin wood slats of the rail.

Later, you keep the phone on. The feeling you carry is familiar: a tense rest, a light on-call sleep because the phone might ring.

Laughed Until We Cried

Up to 70 percent of Parkinson's patients experience some form of dementia as the disease progresses.[5] Some dementia patients like Mom hallucinate and experience paranoia and other psychotic manifestations. Meds can help, but in Mom's case, their help is limited.

Twice, she left the apartment in the middle of the night, convinced Dad was trying to kill her. When she fled, we did not know if she ran into the street and was hit by a car. We did not know if she fell and was lying unconscious at the bottom of the stairs. We did not know if she was curled up like a baby under the pool table on the mezzanine, or if she was sitting in the room next to the vending machine, ready for a midnight snack.

The first time, Drew found her crouched in the stairwell between the third and fourth floors of their building. The second time, she left their unit and we found her in someone else's apartment kitchen. The couple who lived there had the lights on and were sitting up with her. Mom had asked them to call the police.

The officers arrived and interviewed Mom. She told them that Dad was working with a "whole organization of men" to harm her. Drew arrived and told the police, as if it wasn't clear, that she was paranoid and psychotic. He reassured the officers that she was safe and that Dad would not hurt her. We were trying to help her.

I thought about looking at Facebook message boards for advice about cognitive decline and psychosis, but I found them to be either too sad to read or so depressing they bordered on humor.

One woman posted on a dementia caregiving group chat: "Merry Christmas? Dad sat in front of the TV for the past 15 minutes asking for help from actors in drug ads."

One man, in dry seriousness, shared, "I want to know something. I've put my entire life aside to care for my mom with dementia. Will I ever get my life back?" Some things are so sad that you have to laugh so they don't undo you. At this man's comment, Drew and I laughed until we cried.

When the phone rang in the middle of the night, it did not look like a movie scene in which there is a once-in-a-decade call from a relative sharing the news that an uncle had died from a stroke or a grandfather had passed in the old folks' home in Florida. We were on a long, slow road of degeneration. The night calls came often, and one or the other of us would get dressed and drive ten minutes to the apartment where they insisted on living independently while needing frequent help.

Sometimes Mom did not leave the apartment but was wide awake, agitated, and scared. I would arrive and rub her calves. Give her sips of water. A cube of ice on her tongue. Laps with the walker to the bathroom.

On these nights, I often think of the times when Jesus healed. I cannot heal like Agnes or the man who put his hot hands on Rupe. I can help, but just a little. Healing itself is so visceral: Jesus made mud by mixing his spit with dirt and smeared the paste over a blind man's eyes. Mary broke the perfume balm over Jesus's feet. She dried her tears over his feet with her hair.

When mom is sundowning, she is on an entirely different plane. She is in her own reality. I wonder what it looks like in her head.

One night, I drove to pick up my parents and found Mom roaming past a Domino's Pizza with Dad. She was pushing her walker around kids at a skate park and a cluster of tents pitched by people who were unhoused. She was spitting out vitriolic things, confused and mean. Her small chest appeared puffed, a ruffled bird on defense. Light as a feather but hardened.

Sometimes, when I would get angry at God, I would yell in the car, alone. I was trying to release something too tangled up to unwind. Anger was a sheet covering deep fear. Was I supposed to be at peace at the same time I was witnessing my mother's unraveling?

My friend Tony reminded me that I do not know how to do this because I've never done it before. If your loved one is in an altered state and you are not a mental health professional or physician, how could you know where to begin? If you are, for example, a mechanic, a dental hygienist—or, God help you, a writer—it's just you and family and friends trying to figure out how to help, one day at a time.

In calmer moments, I asked myself how I was feeling. Mom is not OK. Dad is not OK. *Was I OK?* I tried to pray, but it was difficult. I managed to ask God to meet her in a small, clear space in her mind, even if it was one we could not see.

If there were no clear spaces, I asked God to meet Mom in a cloudy one. To unravel the tangle of confusion and fear, to bring some relief in the theater of her mind, whatever film was on repeat. Her thoughts, I imagined, looked like flying over a city covered in fog. Sometimes, in thinner places, a small light emerged.

Raham

The Hebrew word for "compassion" is *raham*, which is closely related to the Hebrew word for "womb"[6] (they share the same three-letter root but with different vowels). Raham conveys a deep and nurturing kind of compassion.

In pregnancy, an increased amount of blood flows through the mother's head. The blood-brain barrier is more porous, spongier. By nine weeks, the baby's brain is visible, a tiny squiggle of gluey flesh. In labor, the mother's brain releases more chemicals to help her cope with pain. The nervous system is typically a mother's friend. An interior doula, coaching her through.

Mom's brain, which grew from squiggle to girl to mother and carried my baby brain through the same cycle, is withering. It's unbearable to think about it. Mom's body is also failing. At eighty-four pounds, she received a "severe malnutrition" diagnosis and was scanned for possible tumors to explain the rapid loss of body weight. Her tests and blood work were clear; she was simply not eating.

I tell myself, gently, that I am doing the best I can. I am anxious and awkward in my care, but my *raham* is growing.

Once, in a lucid moment at the kitchen table, Mom told me that sometimes she wants to run in the yard, take her clothes off, and scream. Her brain is trapping her, she said. That is how it feels to lose your cognition. You want to strip naked and scream loud enough until your brain snaps back in your head. I just want to be her kid again.

6

Caregiving

Everyone grows up at a certain age. For me, it was five years ago, at forty-two. I stopped talking about aging with any hint of irony at forty-two. I did not use the word "adulting" any longer.

The language shift started when I became a caregiver for Dad. He got sick with multiple myeloma at the start of the pandemic, and two years later he had a stroke that caused him to fall and break his hip. I cared for him in my own way. My own way is highly administrative, sometimes tender, but rarely patient. I cared for him because I loved him and sometimes because I wanted to, but at other times, as an only child, because I had to. With no holy hyssop to cleanse the calcifications forming on my mother's brain, her Parkinson's-induced cognitive and physical changes meant she could comfort Dad but not practically care for him. There was no one else but me and Drew.

After the casserole season of caregiving, when text threads from concerned family and friends naturally quieted down, I learned that there is no hermitage to retreat to when you are taking care of someone. It is mundane and logistical, this business of getting sick. The burn-off of any remaining energy happens around the same time church members stop delivering post-surgery lasagnas.

For caregivers, there is no divine pillow that softens the blows that come from anticipating future pain and loss. There may be occasional peace like a river, but left to my own devices there is a generalized anxiety, an avoidance, and a proclivity to self-soothe. There is not the possibility of geographical or emotional removal from care. You are in it, and it is hard.

Like a Dance

Anxious caregivers do manage to sometimes get out of their heads for various reasons, and it usually involves providing practical help. Once, I was with Dad for a bone marrow biopsy at a cancer center in Seattle. On the way to his procedure room, we passed by many patient and caregiver pairs, couples on a frequently mopped dance floor.

There were no corsages or strappy heels here. But I found these patients and caregivers to be beautiful in a different way. The grace of one person being rolled in a chair, the other doing the rolling. One person buying snacks, the other saying thank you. No one hedging for power or control. No one elbowing their way to the top of an imaginary ladder.

We were all just with someone we love, wheeling them, pulling for them, waiting for them. Or if we were the patient, we were letting ourselves be loved and cared for. Sometimes for a moment or two, in the guise of fear and grief, love manifested. I knew what sort of love it was—the kind that remembers.

When Dad got sick, I told myself that I could care for him either the easy way or the hard way. I realized that I probably picked the hard way much of the time because God felt nearer in affliction. God is easier to forget when things are going well. I noted this behavior and wondered if, in some sense, trouble kept me safe. Did I confuse my *feeling* close to God with *being* close to God?

Coming alongside someone who is sick can reveal the worst parts of us. It did for me. I discovered how little fortification I possess to sustain a sense of peace. When we are one moment away from the next ER visit or a refill run to the overnight pharmacy, even a seasoned caregiver can quickly use up any store of regulated emotions. Instead, we end up in the hospital waiting room wearing a too-big T-shirt and droopy sweats tucked into rain boots, giving the on-call internist a download of our loved one's meds. We wonder if they believe us, we look so wild. We look the way we feel.

Taking care of my parents was not optional, but I did not feel trapped. The care was a response to circumstances no one could have predicted or controlled. In a natural disaster, you don't have the luxury of time to write a pro-and-con list before helping your neighbor; you just start cleaning up. Yes, there was no one else to take care of my parents besides me and Drew, but that fact did not suffocate us. It's a terrible thing to suffer alone. I would not want to suffer alone, and I did not want to model that kind of abandonment to my kids or peers.

I loved my parents, and that was the reason I cared for them. Still, at times throughout their illnesses, I asked myself, Is taking care of a person more for them, for us, or for God? In my case, I waded through the cloudy water of my interior motivations. In truth, it was an inky mix of all three.

Daddy Hugs

I inherited three things from Dad: anxiety, quick thinking, and the type-A gift of getting stuff done. After Dad was diagnosed, I learned about myeloma clinical trials, found the right specialists, scheduled appointments, and dosed out pills. I kept a document on my phone and another one on my computer with his medical history. I updated our extended family in text threads and peppered in a few lighter comments: "Dad was really craving fried chicken today!" or "I could have earned an associate degree in caregiver management by now!"

I was worried about the genetic link of myeloma between parent and child, and per usual I became fixated on the state of my own body, scanning for symptoms that aligned with Dad's. I felt guilty about this compulsion, also per usual, and it became a frequent topic in therapy. How could a caregiver try to control the situation by turning the gaze of concern toward herself? By following a well-worn, lifelong pattern, that's how.

My desire for control also manifested in other ways. Like millions of other people who had immunocompromised loved ones during the pandemic, I tried to keep Dad safe. One Tuesday in May, I drove him to the cancer center for eight hours of treatment in a new trial, taking our usual Covid precautions. I brought the hand gel, held the door, and made sure his mask stayed above his nose.

Spending time with Dad during his illness was rarely reflective. Between Dad's appointments, there was some comic relief, maybe we watched something stupid on TV. But most days, there was little time to connect. I worked full-time, wrote, and with Drew took care of two kids and tried to take care of my parents.

There were no strolls around the reservoir trail near the house, Dad shuffling with a walker and me pacing by his side, placing a soft blanket over his shoulders. We were functioning, surviving. His anxiety became mine in those months, my body a sponge for his worry. Instead of relational bonding, I thought about Covid hiding on elevator buttons, knobs, railings, and gasoline pumps. The labor—physical and emotional—of keeping someone you love alive.

On the way home from an appointment, we walked past a gift shop with a board book called *Daddy Hugs* on display in the window. On the cover, a large fox was hugging a fox cub. I do not have that kind of father. He brought me up less "daddy hugs" and more "rapture ready." Still, somehow there was both a lot of fear and a lot of love in our relationship. When I was young, Dad tried to protect me in his own way. Now we're both older, and I try to protect him. Neither of us knew what we were doing, but we were giving it what we had.

Silver Alert

My parents and I toured an assisted living facility for the first time a year into Dad's illness. In such a facility, my parents would have to check in and check out when coming or going. This rule, above all others, my father hates. He is nothing if not independent. They would be required to wear step trackers on strings around their necks. If they once got lost, they would now be found. If they fell or drove away on a delusional mission to get me to school because I am, in their mind that day, ten years old and late for the bell at Saint John's Elementary, they would be identified in the system as outside of the building. *Silver alert.*

There were St. Patrick's Day necklaces and streamers on a table outside of the activity room on the day we visited. A banner with tiny leprechauns cheered up a blank wall with its metallic green flourishes. We scanned a menu and looked inside the dining room, a cafeteria-style space with four-tops. Someone was playing pop radio in the back, prepping for dinner: corned beef and cabbage.

Mom and Dad could opt for a room service add-on, where someone slides a table to their door so they can eat dinner alone. The marketer giving us the tour made it sound like a date night. There is a hairstylist on-site. There is a podiatrist who comes once a month to clip toenails, a miserable job I previously agreed to perform for my father's one remaining baby toenail. He would drive up to the house unannounced, text me that he'd arrived with jumbo clippers, and ask me to gingerly snip.

There are other perks of the assisted living community. Someone cleans your room once a week. Someone does your laundry once a week. Your pills are brought to your door three times a day, which diminishes a sense of medical agency but practically is a real plus. Dad's weekly pill box, which we used to fill, contained rounds and cylinders in shades of pure white, blue-white, and pink-white. Vitamins molded into shapes like tiny fruits only sometimes got taken.

Money was also a stress factor in deciding whether to move into assisted living, specifically how little they had. In this world of care, $100,000 is a drop in the bucket. We are not talking about fancy senior living dining rooms: grasshopper cocktails and rolls with molded butter balls. They would need at least half a million dollars to bankroll the Ritz of sixty-five-plus living. The option we toured was a single-patty-with-fries assisted living situation—a McMansion, fake nice but clean, next to an abandoned parking lot.

"We wanted to leave it all to you, Sara." Mom tells me this without understanding they barely have enough money to qualify for a Medicaid spend-down. I learned that in some assisted living facilities, if you can afford to pay for a couple of years out of pocket, you can apply for Medicaid when you need certain physical assistance, and your savings shrink enough so the government takes over payments. *And my parents keep saying they aren't socialists*, I think with a sense of irony. If we can get them into an assisted living facility, it will cost everything they have, but they will be able to stay.

We stood in the parking lot for a long time after the tour. "It's a lot to process, moving from living independently to checking in and out of a place," I told them. "There is so much that's good about it, like not having to clean or make food. But . . ."

"It feels like the final step," Mom finished my sentence. "Like this is it."

Dogs and Horses

Some people keep going in the face of challenges because they're stubborn or they have gumption—some inner will surfaces. My father keeps going because he is anxious. His anxiety propels him forward. It is an arrow, a slingshot, and sometimes an addiction.

Dad's gambling habit turned into a full-blown addiction by the time I was in preschool. I started spending the weekend days with him at dog and horse tracks when we would visit family in Chicago.

Dad's four siblings scattered to both coasts after high school, a great Indiana diaspora of the 1970s. The fifth and only sibling who remained in the state, Dad enrolled in undergrad for a couple of years at a nearby university before he dropped out. He eventually started a business that made some money. By the '80s he had found a way to make more money than he knew what to do with. He began to gamble because he is compulsive and anxious and probably also because he didn't have many friends. Even a sad off-track betting community is a community.

And let me tell you, the off-track betting place near the Fort Wayne Mall was one of the saddest places a person could go. The racetrack in Chicago was a close second. The ground around the barred-up little window where you go to place bets was littered with discarded tickets, confetti from the horses that did not win, place, or show.

Dad would go through periods of giving up gambling, stretches lasting a couple of weeks to a couple of years. He would confess to church elders, to Mom, and sometimes to me in the living room. He occasionally attended Gamblers Anonymous meetings. He would usually get upset if Mom asked him how it was going. Sometimes, guilt at the surface of his emotions made him erupt with sarcasm and anger. He told me he gambled on my college graduation day, on my wedding day, and any "happy day" he read as lucky.

Dad was buoyant and social at church, wearing tailored suits and helping pass the offering tray during a stint as a deacon. At home, he sulked and watched TV in the dark. Home Dad and Church Dad were like living with an actor. Sunday showtime for Church Dad was 11:00 a.m., and by the time the Chicago Bears game came on at 1:00 p.m., Home Dad was back, his spirits lifting or falling with each three-point conversion.

Dad often went to regional casinos, including "the gambling boat," one of several casino cruises that floated off the coast of Lake Michigan with the Chicago skyline in view. He bet with help from a bookie on football, baseball, and basketball games. Once or twice a week, he dropped by a travel agency to pick up or drop off envelopes because the owner, Peg, was married to the bookie. I never saw the bookie but his name was Stan, and in my mind he was huge.

He could bloody you up if you didn't pay. Dad told me, "This kind of guy wears brass knuckles and can break bones." No doubt, this knowledge added to his anxiety. I wondered, naturally, if the bookie's men would come after me, and this made me anxious too. It was an era when there were kidnappings in the news, such as Jaclyn Dowaliby, the seven-year-old a state over who was about my age when she was abducted from her bedroom one night. Or Tara Calico, who about a week later was abducted in New Mexico while riding her bike.

Starter Salad

The bookie was real, but the most anxiety-inducing men in my young life lived in my imagination. Before she met

Dad, Mom met a boy named Joe who got her pregnant at sixteen. She would have the baby in a home two states over, operated by Catholic Charities, and her infant son would go on to be adopted. My grandfather was named Joseph, but I never knew him. My middle name is Jo after him, a feminine version of Joe. There were a lot of Josephs and Marys in the Italian Catholic neighborhoods of Chicago. Every Italian in Bridgeport seemed to have someone in the family connected to the mafia, and we heard the same mob stories each year over Christmas dinner.

Throughout large portions of the 1970s and '80s, Rich, my cousin Danny's friend, would drive from Chicago to my grandparents' lake house near the Illinois border on summer weekends to get wasted on Pabst and shoot fireworks off the pier. When Danny got married at a downtown church in the late '80s and had a reception at a nearby hotel, members of the wedding party were called into the room while guests cheered. I was in the wedding party as a preteen, which qualified me as a "junior" bridesmaid. I wore a dark silver dress with a big poof on one sleeve and bigger hair-sprayed bangs.

None of the actual bridesmaids wanted to walk in with Rich, who was sloppily drunk by the time the reception began. I was tasked with looping my arm around Rich's elbow as we lined up outside the banquet hall. "Now let's welcome groomsman Rich and junior bridesmaid Sara!" the MC called. The doors fanned open, and we moved toward a few hundred guests to a front table. Woozy and unable to stand, Rich slammed his weight into me after a few steps. My free hand smashed into a guest's starter salad. Mortified and heart racing, I ran to Mom. "Oh, Richard was just joking around, Sara," she said, shrugging me off and turning back to her table.

In my head, alcoholism and gambling were equally vicious addictions. Rich, wasted and smashing my hand into the wedding guest's side salad, had the same root malady as Dad, who worried about getting his fingers smashed if he did not drop off his envelope at the travel agency.

We all seemed exposed, at risk of being on the wrong side of reckless men. Men tearing into sandwiches at Al's #1 Italian Beef with one hand, chugging Old Style Lager with the other. I spent my adolescence suspicious and on guard.

Fake Dad

Men at the church in my Indiana hometown were not like Rich, at least not on Sunday mornings. They were dads and wore suits and wacky ties with Looney Tunes characters or sports team logos. They were well-groomed and held the door. The male pastors and elders of my youth were measured and not hot-tempered in public. We church kids watched them from the coffee and donut table in the fellowship hall after Bible study.

Later in life, beginning in undergrad, I found a different set of men who were more interesting than church dads because they were bookish. They were in touch and aware, gentle and thoughtful, and I wanted them to be my Fake Dad. I wanted to wear flannels and fly-fish with these Fake Dads or go to a literary festival with them. I wanted us to do crosswords and talk about the classics.

On campus, professors, a version of Fake Dads, were often the center of a circle of students on the quad. They were *spiritual* but never evangelical. They were corduroyed and tweedy. They loved Edward Abbey and Wendell Berry. They usually threw Annie Dillard into the mix. I learned from these men that there comes a time in life when the identities of evangelical and aesthete cannot coexist, and one or the other must give. By the time I got to undergrad, an aspiring English major without a family of origin who modeled deep thinking, I needed these men to affirm me.

I was not attracted to these professor-types sexually because they occupied a place in my thinking reserved for the paternal. They were Fake Dads. However, at times there was a realization that I could still leverage the power of my soft-skinned youth with the almost-senior set if I were to decide to become, say, another person for some reason. Any mild attraction to professors ended when I noticed how the legs of these men changed. Once lean mountain climber and cyclist legs, there was a frailty you could see in their crossed legs on stage at the lecture hall that threw cool water on any passing thought of a liaison.

Boomers had given up hippie culture for subdivisions; at least a lot of them had. But some had become intellectuals. I idealized the lives of these bookish men and imagined the moment they fled to a cabin—or a large foursquare in walking distance of a Midwestern liberal arts college—and stacked their books in arty piles. We all wanted to hang out in their offices or sleep on the rug or chaise lounge next to their desks. At its heart, my attraction was academic, generally spiritual, and paternal. I wished instead there were women in my life to fill these roles: academic, generally spiritual, and maternal.

Except for a high school journalism teacher who hung a photograph she'd taken of a young Chelsea Clinton walking down the street with Bill above her desk. This teacher had strapped herself to a tall oak outside our classroom window one year when workers were about to cut it down. There were no other independent women like this in my young life. Everyone was a housewife or a burned-out working mother. No women I knew when I was coming up had the leisure of a thought life or centered their day around a creative practice while someone else took care of the kids and house.

Fake Dads were not anxious like Dad. In my imagination, any anxiety they had was about the demise of the independent bookstore, a threat to salmon from a proposed watershed, or nuclear annihilation. Their anxiety was issues-based and broad; it was nothing like mine.

My anxiety lived in my body and was about my body. I was worried about my body because Dad was worried about my body. He took me to the pediatrician frequently. We kept Dr. Wade Adams in business. Pink, powdery Amoxil was in our fridge next to the milk come winter. My anxiety was Dad's, and it tasted like bubblegum.

In an episode of the television series *Julia*, about the life of Julia Child, there is a line she delivers about her father that I had to immediately write down. "I am who I am because of him and in spite of him."[1] This was true for her, and it's true for me. We are who we are because of our parents and despite our parents, in the presence or absence of them.

Finally, Covid

Dad and Mom got Covid after they moved into the assisted living facility in the winter of early 2024, almost four years after the coronavirus first arrived in Washington State assisted living facilities before anywhere else in the US. I started calling Rite Aid and Bartell Drug locations across the greater Seattle metro area, asking if they had doses left of the antiviral Paxlovid, which Dad especially needed because he was immunocompromised from chemo. "Call Kirkland," one pharmacist said. "Try Queen Anne," said the next. "Or West Seattle and Bitter Lake." There was a Paxlovid shortage, and no pharmacist I talked to knew when more doses might arrive.

I found a dose the next day at the cancer center pharmacy where Dad was treated and texted him, telling him to take three pills after I dropped them off outside his door. I called an hour later to make sure Dad took the first dose of three pills. "Yes, I did," he said. I called him that night, reminding him to take his second round of three pills. "I only took one pill earlier," he said. "You just told me to take one, didn't you?"

I exploded at him on the phone. Did he want me to come over, "get Covid, and hand-feed him the three pills? This is life or death." I swore and hung up.

I felt terrible for the next couple of days, even after apologizing, and talked to my therapist, Sara, about what happened. "I don't know if I'm angry or afraid," I said.

Sara reminded me that anger is often secondary to a raw, base emotion. In my case, fear. "Anger feels more empowering," she said, "and engaging with fear is deeply uncomfortable. But being hard on yourself about losing it with your dad is not going to help. Instead, try to extend compassion. If you want to not explode, you have to accept you're not in control of your dad's health. It's not up to you to keep your parents alive." At this, I felt an immense relief. I heard an invitation to accept the reality of their illness and exhale.

7

Embodiment

The warm, spicy smell of tomato leaves. The first time Drew and I held each other, standing in a breezeway connecting the student commons to his dorm. Dry juniper air in eastern Oregon. Drew's laugh-cry face the moment Asher was born. The bend on a Seattle highway when Mount Rainier appears, taking up half the sky: The first time I saw it, I didn't know what else to do except scream.

These are embodied moments. They connect the natural, spiritual, and emotional. They don't cost any money. They are fleeting and sometimes surprising. They are often relational, experienced with another person or within creation.

The adrenaline that ran through my body when an ultrasound technician snapped ten images of the same spot on my breast. The call that Dad has multiple myeloma. Breaking news alerts. The tail of a rat, visible from a closet trap. A friend waking me up to say the South Tower had fallen on September 11, 2001: That morning, I watched black-and-white images of the buildings collapsing on our old television dozens of times in a row.

These are anxious moments. Micro or global, reconciled or unending, they can take over quickly. Sometimes, a surge of adrenaline courses through the body to the gut before the brain can think.

In the anxious moments of the years leading up to, during, and following the pandemic, I spent my days taking care of my family: my parents, my husband, my children. Besides anxiety, avoidance and guilt were often present in the care I provided. My usual pattern of getting emotional hangovers from absorbing their anxiety, then checking out to cope, was grinding me down. At one point, I tried skin smoothies and hydrotherapy to find some small relief, but these, of course, failed to answer my deeper spiritual questions of why I could not sustain peace and why my body was wrecked. Something had to change.

I wanted to experience the body as a place where God works in the presence of fatigue and worry about our own life, the lives of people we love, and the world. Instead of numbing out or trying another wellness remedy that would inevitably fail, I needed to understand something about embodiment.

What Embodiment Is

I don't know how to understand Christianity without considering the body. Christians believe that humankind was created in God's image—in physical bodies. This must mean God can meet us through the body, just like God can meet us when we go out into nature through our experience of the created world.

In Christianity, embodiment is the belief that all people are made in the image of God and that the spirit, soul, and body are connected. The incarnation offers us a way to think theologically about embodiment. The doctrine teaches that Jesus was fully God and fully human. This incarnate Jesus, embodied in flesh, slept, sang, laughed, ate, and suffered. And in the end, God promises that all who love him—in bodies of every color, age, and condition—will be made new. The body will not be lost or shaken off; the resurrected body will be with God eternally.

In anthropological terms, embodiment is "a way of describing porous, visceral, felt, enlivened bodily experiences, in and with inhabited worlds."[1] The subset "biblical anthropology" is interested in how Christians "discern the resonances, places of continuity and discontinuity" between biblical texts and "how they present to us a vision of what it means to be human."[2] But instead of through human behavior or theology, I wanted to understand how embodiment is practiced in community.

I more closely related to psychologist Hillary McBride's definition of embodiment: "The experience of being a body in a social context" that often "comes with a particular kind of ache, liberation, or both, depending on whether the person experienced body violation, illness, or pain."[3] McBride is interested in how we can become healthier and more present through embodied practices and lists qualities that are required along the way: "curiosity, attention, sensation, and acceptance, which then allows us to develop a healthier and more stable relationship with our body as a whole."[4] I realized that my own bodily curiosity, attention, and sensations are often bent toward what might be wrong with my body. I had not been able to accept my body or maintain stability in my relationship to it because the majority of my explorations have been driven by fear and to avoid suffering.

The Reality of the Body

It's easier for embodiment to hover as a theoretical concept when you are physically healthy and are not trying to find relief from pain or illness in your body. Although arguably when pain is staring us in the face, embodiment as a practice becomes more essential. It's also easier to talk about embodiment when you are of a dominant racial, gender, sexual, and socioeconomic identity. As McBride notes, "While for some of us it may take an event—a serious illness or a trauma—to remember that we are bodies, many people do not have to wait for a specific event to remember the centrality of their body. That's because their body is placed outside the cultural hierarchy of the 'ideal body,' and so they learn early on that their body makes them 'other.'"[5] I read this and realized the many ways I have been exceptionally privileged, that my own lack of embodiment is internally cultivated and not put upon me by oppressive power structures.

Anthropologically and theologically, embodiment makes sense. But I found that, probably because I've become skeptical of the way wellness culture is attached to embodiment as a *vibe*, I had become resistant and hesitant to adopt the kind of embodiment that leads to acceptance of my exceptionally average but perfectly healthy body. Eventually, I realized I was just being defensive because practicing embodiment would force me to handle the awkward and detached parts of myself I would prefer not to touch. I started to differentiate between embodied wellness culture, which was a by-product of capitalism sold by influencers, and practices for spiritual and physical well-being.

As a girl, I was taught that my body is a thing to criticize by watching Mom and my grandmother criticize their bodies. I've seen women I love get sick and become thin as rails. They dieted their entire lives, Jane Fonda–style. They thigh mastered and calorie counted, and then they got a diagnosis and shriveled to eighty-four pounds. They became so small you could not look straight at them because you loved them and saw them starting to disappear from age and illness.

I recently told a friend as we passed a bakery stand at a farmers market that I'm back on carbs. I gave them up in the 2000s, I told her, but I don't know why. "Everyone stopped eating carbs in the 2000s," she joked. I now start each day with the simple pleasure of toast and jam.

Back when illness and caregiving for Mom and Dad were theoretical, I rarely thought about the aging body. Now, after all that has happened with my parents, I want to enjoy every bite. To eat well while I can. The practices of eating slowly and thinking about color and texture are a kind of embodiment that leads to a deeper acceptance, even gratitude, for the body.

But beyond the physical, there's something about my anxious disposition that remains stuck when practicing embodiment—be it stretching, intentionally breathing, or moving my body in a way that draws me to the present. It's difficult to change from a default fast pace, even one that is not helpful. If I was calm, present, and engaged, would I lose some imaginary edge? And did I have to be *earthy* to be embodied?

I wonder, why does the stereotype I have of an embodied person often look like a certain kind of female? I visualize a barefoot woman wearing a flowy skirt, swaying in a forest bath—sitting still in nature and engaging all of her senses. To be embodied, did I need to look the part? Would I need to begin wearing neutral, layered linen and oversized earrings?

In all honesty, I am deeply uncomfortable, yet in some way envious, of what I imagine as the modern embodied woman. I started to realize how many cultural stereotypes I have of this person. Maybe she is a ceramicist in Joshua Tree and gets her photo taken on rocky crags. She can look at the camera with a serious face. The kind of face that says I have a body, and I have accepted it, and it happens to be beautiful. I could just as easily be naked, but I chose instead to wear a strappy tank top.

I wonder if it is easier to be embodied if your face is symmetrical, your skin creamy smooth, and your eyebrows full. Like learning a second language or how to drive a stick shift, it's harder to learn this sort of embodiment when you are no longer young.

Stuck Places

I was referred to a massage therapist after a fender bender several years ago. "Tell Ruth what you'd like," the person scheduling my appointments said over the phone, "because . . . she has her own style." I soon learned what the scheduler meant after arriving at Ruth's office in a windowless room in an office building. I lay on my back as she began to feel around my rib cage and abdomen. "Your liver is stuck," she said, poking around my stomach. "Turn toward me a little more," she instructed, cupping her hand like a bowl. "I can almost get under the ribs and move the heart. Turn on your stomach, let me feel your kidneys."

There were many organs mentioned during the hour; I had a lot of stuck places. I made myself laugh the session off because the idea of Ruth manually adjusting my spleen, of really thinking about the fact that I have organs ticking and circulating and expanding with air, was unnerving. Was Ruth being embodied a requirement for her to feel when an organ was bound by emotion or immobile from anxiety? If so, I wasn't interested.

What did interest me was less the wellness-tinged versions of embodiment that equate wholeness with "taking up space" and more the embodiment practiced by Jesus when he was suffering in a broken body. What I've found in liturgical traditions is a vocabulary for suffering. Jesus died, and his body was smeared with a spice paste and wrapped tightly in linen. Because I was in a time with death hovering near and far, I wanted to understand as much as I could about it. *Maybe,* I thought, *if I let myself ponder death, I will be able to become more embodied in my life.*

Contemplating Death

I allowed myself to begin thinking about death instead of avoiding all thoughts about it. I had the privilege of health and a little perspective after the worst of the pandemic and the first years of my parents' diagnoses had passed. Helping with their care was a new normal, and I'd fallen into enough of a rhythm that I could reflect on the years prior. I also had not grieved them yet, and there was still a slight idealism that I tapped into to feign control over their future passings.

And so I began. I prayed through an Ignatian "death contemplation"—a way of imagining what death could look like to move toward holy indifference about it—and journaled about my ideal death. I wrote an obituary for myself to see how I would want to be remembered. The more I allowed myself to think about death, the more death became curious instead of scary. Like having a baby or entering perimenopause, death is something you can learn about. It can slip from one side of your mind, the emotional part that flares the nervous system, to the logical side. There, it becomes just another thought. Today, I might be reading an article on Haiti, writing a shopping list, or thinking about death. Death, the idea of dying, became an interesting object to turn over in my palm and look at from different angles.

Around this time, I purchased a copy of *The Art of Dying Well* at my neighborhood bookstore. You should have seen the face of the salesperson, who turned her default frown into more of a gentle pout when I handed her my selection. Anyone buying a book about "dying well" demands a softened sympathy, even from the most literarily austere clerk.

I learned practical tips from reading—bring electric tea lights into the hospital room when your loved one is dying and ask to turn down the overhead lights. When your loved one has died and their death was not spontaneous but has come after a period of hospice care, do not call 911. The responders will treat the matter like an emergency. Take several moments, then call the county coroner and report an expected death.[6]

I developed a deep admiration for death doulas, who along with hospice nurses became the people least like me that I most wished I could emulate. I read about death doulas who served crucial roles in Ukraine during the Russian invasion, where two-thirds of citizens had lost a loved one in the first years of the conflict. In addition to coming alongside people who lost family and friends in the war, Ukrainian death doulas worked with people who fled their homes, lost jobs and income, or experienced other traumas. Each was a kind of death that happens when we are still alive.[7]

I thought of Jesus who interestingly had a death that was both expected and unforeseen. His death did not come after illness but resulted from brutality. He knew it was going to happen, and he also knew he would descend into hell, proclaiming victory over death, before returning to Earth for a little while and ascending to heaven in a new body. He knew it would only hurt for *a little while*. None of us have knowledge about the hour of our death, but Jesus did. I imagine Mary as a maternal comforter at her son's birth and a death doula at the foot of the cross, bearing witness and empathy at her son's crucifixion. Sitting in these scenes in prayer made the life of Jesus more real and his death more palpable.

Jesus didn't have to be born in a stable; he was born like an animal, with other animals. The devil would have been well served to remember how Jesus came to earth when he was tempting him in the desert. He didn't know Jesus at all when he offered him the cities of the world in exchange for Jesus's allegiance. Mary could have told him it was futile. She knew her son.

I wanted that kind of love for my kids. The kind that loves them no matter what happens in the future. I wanted to be the kind of kid my mom and dad could love like that.

Discipline and Sacramentalism

Jesus "made himself nothing by taking the very nature of a servant, being made in human likeness" (Phil. 2:7). Jesus became embodied and denied himself relief. No angels plucked him off "the hard wood of the cross."[8] Instead, he lived alongside his friends bringing purpose and dignity, but he did not remove their uncertainty.

Jesus used his body to model spiritual disciplines such as fasting, prayer, worship, and rest. These practices are meant to be *practiced*. They help to ground us in the present in our bodies and to accept that we don't know what any day will hold.

Anxiety is held in our bodies. So is worship, breath, and stillness. Practicing these bodily postures helps release anxiety and better fortifies us to do good work in the world. Dallas Willard writes, "We have to involve the body in spiritual formation because that is where we live and what we live from. . . . Spiritual formation is the formation of the 'inner' dimensions of the human being, resulting in a transformation of the whole person, including the body in its social context. Spiritual formation is never merely inward, but is always also explosively outward."[9] Christians are invited to be formed by remaining proximate to Jesus through practicing disciplines that mold us into embodied, present people who can hold ambiguity and uncertainty. This is because Jesus modeled how to do so in his life on earth. Willard is right. If we are well-formed but don't do anything to serve other people, what's the point?

While thinking one day about the intersection between anxiety, God, and the body, the term "somatic theology" came to mind. I wondered for a moment if I was onto something new. "Google it," Drew said, making coffee before a meeting. "It sounds like you're actually talking about sacramentalism." I googled it, and he was right. There was already a word for the thing I was trying to define.

God uses sacraments to ground us in a deeper story. Writer Tsh Oxenreider said, "We are body-soul composites, and we often need our bodies to tell our souls true things until we believe them."[10] Sacramentalism is a way for the Christian to practice embodiment. The sacraments—including communion and baptism—tangibly remind Christians that we are made to love God and be loved back. Through the sacraments, God meets us substantially in physical creation.

Jesus says mysterious things about his body. He is the bread of life. His body and blood are taken in communion. No matter what you think about transubstantiation, whether or not the actual body and blood of Jesus are on offer, I would gladly dip a real body of Christ wafer into the cup and put it on my tongue. We need as much of Christ's body on earth as we can get. Taking the physical markers of God's presence seriously through the sacraments brings Christians more into the body and less into the moment.

Casting Off the Yoke of Worry

Embodiment is different from gnosticism. One of the key beliefs in gnosticism is dualism, the idea that matters of the mind and the spirit are higher than the body. In contrast, sacramentalism makes room for an embodied sense—God works *through* our minds and bodies. The apostle Paul's letters, for example, would have been different if someone else had written them, in part because the author would have lived in a different body.

Dualism holds little appeal to me. I am a twenty-first-century American, not a Greek thinker in the first century. Neoplatonism and gnosticism were common ideologies then. It was the culture. People talked about Plato, and Plato talked about caves, not flesh. Still, like many peers, I was taught to deprioritize the importance of my body. It was us against desire.

A lot of kids raised in evangelicalism were taught to keep the body in check because it was dangerous and needed to be controlled and monitored. I was told as a teen that the body could get pregnant, get drunk and drive, kiss and get mono, or step on a "dirty needle" at a park and get HIV. I was often on high alert.

Theologian W. David O. Taylor recalled that when he was growing up, "the body was at best a neutral thing that you just shuffled around. At worst it is something to be feared because it is going to somehow, by its very nature . . . pervert our ability to love God and to worship God faithfully. So it was something to be feared, mistrusted, suppressed, transcended, tortured, tamed." Taylor instead argues that God has "something better on offer for us that is truly, deeply good news for everyone, because we are all bodily."[11]

Learning to temper anxiety about the body by practicing spiritual disciplines and sacramentalism may take a lifetime, but encountering the freedom the practices bring can be magnificent because, as Taylor says, "the Holy Spirit is the author of all flesh coming alive with a Jesus-like radiance.

. . . Our bodies are these ambulatory tabernacles that carry around the goodness and grace and life and holiness of Jesus everywhere we go. . . . So we are ourselves these sacramental sites."[12]

My worried body is far from a sacramental site, but I want to experience at least a little of the freedom that embodiment can bring. I start small. In the morning, I pray the daily offering of Thérèse of Lisieux. The nineteenth-century saint asks God to purify her completely, presenting her body, mind, and actions within her daily prayer: *O my God! I desire to sanctify every beat of my heart, my every thought, my simplest works, by uniting them to [his] infinite merits.*[13]

The choice to cast off a yoke of worry and stay close and present with God in our bodies, with their limits and pressing anxieties, is a daily thing. But days to weeks, weeks to months, months to years, we can grow small deposits of calm that sustain us.

PART TWO

THE CHURCH BODY

8

Scrupulosity

One of the first concerts I attended after Covid quarantine was with the singer-songwriter Adrianne Lenker at Washington Hall, a small historic venue in central Seattle. Looking around, I spotted one man in the balcony with gray hair, but at forty-four I was unquestionably one of the oldest people in the room. From another quick scan of the crowd, I could guess that most were members of Gen Z. As I watched them listen to the music, I was drawn to their earnestness, awkwardness, and aesthetic, which looked a lot like the way I dressed in the '90s as a Gen X teen.

I felt an almost maternal interest in this generation. I was already personally invested. As a mother, I had recently begun to walk with my son through a new mental health diagnosis. And like a lot of parent peers, I started to read about the massive wave of generational anxiety and mental health crises centered on young people coming out of the pandemic, both in and outside of the church.

Anxious Generations

"Asher, you're such a screenager," my daughter, Sabine, told her older brother at dinner one night last year. I snorted and tried not to spit out my water, having never heard "screenager" before. My son survived middle school without a phone because of his concern—and these are his words—"that a phone will corrupt me." There came a point where we needed to be able to contact him at a summer camp, so we bought him a basic phone for texting. He was, it turns out, not a screenager. His sister, on the other hand, was gifted with a smartwatch in sixth grade after asking for months. One kid is an introvert, the other an extrovert. But coming out of the pandemic with online church and remote learning, they—like their peers—were both starved for real, in-person social interactions.

Experts talk about loneliness using words like "epidemic" and "disease" and say our cognitive, mental, and physical health suffers when we are isolated. As a kid in the '80s, I heard the surgeon general talk about the dangers of secondhand smoke at a time when people were still allowed to light up on airlines and in hospitals. In 2023, the US surgeon general published the eighty-two-page report, "Our Epidemic of Loneliness and Isolation," which measured our lack of social connection, reporting that "the mortality impact of being socially disconnected is similar to that caused by smoking up to 15 cigarettes a day."[1]

Jonathan Haidt, *The Anxious Generation* author and researcher, wrote in a widely shared *Atlantic* piece that teens today are lonelier and have fewer friends, at least real-life friends, than in previous generations. According to Haidt, "rates of depression and anxiety in the United States—fairly stable in the 2000s—rose by more than 50 percent in many studies from 2010 to 2019."[2] Suicide rates shot up more than 130 percent for girls aged ten to fourteen.[3]

Haidt argues that the culprit of increased teen anxiety is clear: Gen Z is the first generation to adopt smartphones and use social media before parents knew what we were getting into.[4] Statistics showed Christian kids fared better and were less lonely during the pandemic, benefiting from a stronger connection to church communities.[5] I considered these statistics and felt a sense of gratitude for our church, and a sense of urgency that there is a lot more the corporate church can do to offer stability and support to young people on the margins.

Our family is connected at Grace. Decades after our first Sunday there, I'm on the vestry and Drew is on staff. We often receive prayer and experience solidarity as parents from other staff and congregants who are also raising kids in an anxious time. In some small sense, Asher and Sabine remained connected to others during the pandemic because of our church, even though we watched the service on a screen from our couch for more than a year.

Instead of just observing adults talk at coffee hour in a fellowship hall—the limit of my young interaction with adults at the church I grew up in—kids at Grace are more integrated into the service. Our youth pastor and his wife attend performances and games of kids in the youth group when they can. It helps our teens feel seen outside of Sunday and reinforces that their presence is vital to the health of our congregation. Haidt is right, community helps, and a big part of that community is our church.

It's also true, however, that a strong sense of community only goes so far when it comes to mental health. The way kids present in public, at church or at school, often isn't congruent with what surfaces at home.

A New Diagnosis

Asher was diagnosed with obsessive-compulsive disorder in 2021 when he started sixth grade. OCD is an anxiety disorder that typically causes people to have obsessive thoughts and repeat compulsions to try to control those thoughts. Sometimes, people with OCD stay focused on a certain obsession and compulsion, like contamination and perfectionism. Asher's OCD obsessions and compulsions jumped all over the place.

OCD typically latches onto the places of greatest vulnerability in a person, to the things that matter most to them. For example, someone with harm OCD, a fixation that they could hurt themselves or someone else, is often gentle by nature, moving a crane fly off the sidewalk by its papery wings so it doesn't get hurt. Someone with existential OCD might experience derealization—intrusive thoughts that their existence isn't real—or fear their spouse isn't the same person they married but instead lives in a different dimension.

In middle school, Asher decided he wanted to talk about OCD freely and matter-of-factly, addressing his class one period to explain how it might show up at school. He shared with his peers that instead of flipping lights a certain number of times or repeatedly washing his hands, he mostly struggles with intrusive thoughts and scrupulosity: a term for moral or religious OCD. Between 5 and 33 percent of people with OCD are scrupulous, "and the number likely rises to between

50% and 60% in OCD sufferers who come from within very strict religious cultures."[6]

There have been a lot of graces in Asher's journey and mental health diagnosis, including a blooming of confidence and extraordinary empathy. Asher and I discussed my sharing some of his story at length on several occasions. With the same clarity he expressed when talking about OCD with his peers, Asher is comfortable with my writing about his diagnosis. The specifics and details of Asher's experience with OCD are his own. I'm sharing with permission, using a wide-angle view from the lens of parenting a kid with religious OCD.

Little Hells

I read Frederick Buechner's *Telling Secrets* in the same months as Asher's OCD diagnosis emerged. In the memoir, Buechner talks about his daughter's inpatient treatment for anorexia.

> "Perfect love casteth out fear," John writes (1 John 4:18 KJV), and the other side of that is that fear like mine casteth out love, even God's love. The love I had for my daughter was lost in the anxiety I had for my daughter. The only way I knew to be a father was to take care of her, as my father had been unable to take care of me, to move heaven and earth if necessary to make her well, and of course I couldn't do that.[7]

Like Buechner, for a long time my anxiety for my child eclipsed my love for my child. My love for him was big, but my anxiety was bigger. I remember calling a friend whose son also has OCD, sitting on the kitchen floor with my back to a cabinet, emotionally hungover, and feeling outside of my body. "It will get better," she said. I couldn't believe her yet.

After Asher was diagnosed with OCD and my parents were diagnosed with physical illnesses, I began to think about the idea of "little hells." Hell as a concept drives some people to be good. It is used as a tool to control. Some people believe hell is a myth. Some people, like me, believe it is the manifestation of separation from God. "In this world you will have trouble" (John 16:33). In this life there will be little hells. Some people, to be sure, are in real hell on earth. Children in Gaza, refugees living through layers of complex trauma, are in a kind of living hell, as are victims of genocide, extraordinary abuse, and systemic oppression. Our experiences may wither in comparison, but even in safety, we all sometimes bear little hells.

"I was in hell," Buechner writes. "I choose the term hell with some care. Hell is where there is no light but only darkness, and I was so caught up in my fear for her life, which had become in a way my life too, that none of the usual sources of light worked any more, and light was what I was starving for." His life continued. So did mine. I managed to shower, get dressed, and work. I was like Buechner who says, "I read books. I played tennis and walked in the woods. I saw friends and went to the movies. But even in the midst of such times as that I remained so locked inside myself that I was not really present in them at all."[8]

The first months after Asher's diagnosis were like walking in the land of the living holding a little death. The person I grew in my body, whose fat cheeks I kissed as a baby, whom I'd loved every day of his life, would not have it easy.

We needed to learn how to counterintuitively parent him. We had a lot to learn. Common compulsions for many types of OCD are confessing and reassurance seeking. It goes against the grain of intuition to not reassure a child, but with OCD, statements such as "that's never going to happen" are like feeding sugar to yeast. OCD flares the more it is fed. The sinking feeling that Drew and I could only love him through, and the cold fact that we could not fix our child but only offer up a flare gun of love in the dark, would have to be enough.

Looking Within

Since mental health diagnoses such as OCD, ADHD, and autism can be genetic, it's typical for parents to consider if other family members share similar traits or characteristics. For example, the genetic link between parents having anxiety and their kids having anxiety has been repeatedly proven. According to the Association of Child and Adolescent Mental Health, "there is clear evidence that anxiety disorders aggregate in families; one study found that over one-third of children with a clinically anxious parent had an anxiety disorder compared with one-fifth where there is no clinically anxious parent."[9]

I began to pull on the threads myself. I'm not interested in using my kid's experience as a self-diagnostic tool, and I haven't received a formal OCD diagnosis. I've simply become more curious about OCD patterns in my own anxiety story.

My mind shot back to the little bedroom in the Craftsman we lived in a decade ago when Asher was a toddler. A Sunday night, winter. In my memory, I sat with my back against the wall, unable to shake a blasphemous thought about the name of God out of my head. It had seeded in the communion line at church earlier in the day. Pushing it away made it gigantic, this thought. I was weighed down by the full-body feeling that the unforgivable sin—a severely troublesome passage in the New Testament for people with scrupulosity—had been committed. I imagined the Book of Life in literal form, my name erased. I imagined my name vanishing after being engraved on the palm of God's hand (see Isa. 49:16). I confessed these thoughts, almost in real time, to my husband, who was patient but a little perplexed.

Scrupulosity is unreasonable. It's the kind of anxiety that bumps up against superstition. If you're a doubter, the strength to persevere in your relationship with God is severely tested when, ironically, the place where you are supposed to find relief—your relationship with God—is what flares your anxiety. You start running to God, but you are not sure if you are nudged by God's grace and kindness or if you are already too far gone.

From the little bedroom memory, with Asher in the next room coloring, I flashed even further back to another scene, the first time it happened. In New York City, on a Sunday, after attending a service in Midtown. I was on the roof in the West Village with friends, eating sandwiches, and the same blasphemous thought filled my head with a light touch. A tip of a feather swooping into my mind. It looped and repeated for days, weeks. The fear of hell, even with all the talk of heaven, got rooted down deep when I was young. Every few years, usually on a Sunday, this thought loop returned.

A decade later, I realized for the first time that the experience was a manifestation of scrupulosity.

Moral Obsessions

Moral obsessions are not limited to Christianity but can be experienced in any religion, including Buddhism and Hinduism. Interestingly, agnostics and atheists can experience scrupulosity too, concerned "that they were somehow wrong in their belief that there is no higher power and . . . that their decisions throughout life could have somehow offended a higher power."[10]

In therapy, treatment for obsessive thoughts often includes exposure and response prevention (ERP). Exposures are a way of sitting with a trigger until the fear and anxiety around the thought spike and subside. Therapist-guided exposures for religious OCD can be counterintuitive, to put it mildly: doodling on a Bible, tearing out a tissue-paper-thin page of the Psalms, writing 666 on a sheet of paper. I wonder if that last one would have helped me as a child. One of my first memories was tracing 666 on my forehead in preschool after Dad first told me that the Antichrist and the rapture were coming soon. I don't know what caused me to do it; I suppose I acted on an intrusive thought. Gripped with fear, I ran to the backyard to find my mom. I told her I was going to hell and burst into tears.

Eternal damnation was a common fear that I shared with peers who grew up in evangelicalism in the '80s and '90s. But recorded incidents of scrupulosity can be traced much further back in time. Notable leaders from throughout church history probably struggled with scrupulosity, including John

Bunyan, who was "harassed by a curiosity in regard to the 'unpardonable sin' and a prepossession that he had already committed it."[11] Saint Thérèse of Lisieux "had a strong obsession with sin in her younger years, fearing that her every action was offensive to God."[12]

Perhaps better known for self-flagellation, Martin Luther "would go into the confessional and recite the previous day's sins not for five minutes, but for two hours, three hours, sometimes even four hours—reciting in detail every sin he could remember. . . . He would come back from the confessional tormented after spending hours confessing his sins. As soon as he got back to his room, he would remember a sin he had forgotten to confess."[13]

I wondered if scruples were a workplace casualty of sainthood, a common pitfall on the way to holiness. Were they a strange prerequisite? What if we know the names of these figures from church history because of a high devotion that manifested in religious obsession, and we mistook scrupulosity for piety? Either way, God graciously works with what we give him.

Being Seen

In the *Spiritual Exercises*, Saint Ignatius wrote that if the enemy of our soul finds us to be without sin, "he brings him or her to judge as sinful something in which no sin exists."[14] Ignatius authored a series of six notes on scruples, including this warning: "The enemy looks much if a soul is gross or delicate, and if it is delicate, he tries to make it more delicate in the extreme, to disturb and embarrass it more."[15] The most tenderhearted among us are the most at risk of being undone.

While the "gross," or unguarded, soul is more prone to sin, Ignatius argues that scruples are more prone to strike the delicate soul "that seems to see sin where there is no sin."[16] A soul like I see in my kid. The goal, of course, is moderation of the soul so that it is neither too gross nor too delicate. To be neither sloppy in Christian practice nor hyperaware.

I used to think my scrupulous tendencies kept me safe and close to God, just like I falsely believed I could not be near to God if I wasn't in a time of trial or affliction. The problem wasn't God; it was me, or at least my pattern of perception. God was always near, but I did not feel him there unless I was self-constrained or in need. My feelings of want and lack were what kept me close. Said another way: I didn't know how to be close to God when things were going well. Or how to simply allow God to care for me. In a session with my spiritual director, Dan said, "We don't know how to live according to how God sees us." I wanted to be seen without having to perform.

Magical Thinking

Overcome by anxiety and intolerance of uncertainty, scrupulous individuals can "practice their own religion," rooted in rigid logic that can impact how they understand God. I know this way of thinking well. Scrupulous people can also be inclined toward "evident magical thinking."[17]

In OCD terms, magical thinking is believing that what we think—and more precisely what we're afraid of—can come true. But we can also follow a similar thought pattern when we want to believe the opposite: what is true can become untrue.

In *The Year of Magical Thinking*, Joan Didion writes about not wanting to give away her late husband John Dunne's effects, believing that he will need them when he comes back. Maybe, by believing John is not gone, he will return. "*The New York Times* knew. *The Los Angeles Times* knew," Didion writes after Dunne died. "Yet I was myself in no way prepared to accept this news as final: there was a level on which I believed that what had happened remained reversible. That was why I needed to be alone. . . . I needed to be alone so that he could come back. This was the beginning of my year of magical thinking."[18]

For a long time, I wanted my son back, even though he was alive. Though his eyes eventually cleared, they had clouded for some time after his OCD diagnosis. He did not look like himself for at least a year. I quickly realized that I was part of the problem with my anxious love. I was trying to erase his suffering because he's my kid. Instead, I inadvertently was feeding it, and it was enlarging. To help him, I had to understand something about how God works in affliction, even in children.

I needed to step aside and learn how to love Asher in a way that did not avoid uncertainty and that led with care instead of restlessness. In the years ahead, the church would be crucial to him finding belonging and getting out of his head. It would also become a place of stability where we could get a little rest.

9

Stability

I've attended the same church for twenty years. More than a thousand Sundays. Two things are true: We are the gathered body of Christ on earth, and because the church is just that, a bunch of people, we have been hurt or done the hurting a fair number of times between us.

Over the years, there have been healthy seasons at Grace. Some were consequential and formative for the congregation, such as the introduction of contemplative practices in the 2010s. Others were small shifts, such as the addition of a processional and recessional to incorporate more embodied worship. There have also been times when swelling waves of anxiety and grief were palpable, either because of the state of the world or because of something going on inside the sanctuary doors. To be clear, I'm not talking about abuse, narcissism, or embezzlement of church resources. I'm talking about the hurt some congregants and leaders experienced as a result of broken relational dynamics in our early years of membership.

For the first ten years I attended Grace, I was not a deacon, a part of the church's leadership team, or a pastor's wife. I was an anonymous attendee. I was an observer and mostly talked to the same few people on Sundays before leaving as quickly as possible after the service.

It was easy for a person to be anonymous at Grace until they were ready to be known. Maybe people saw me, but they didn't engage with me until I was good and ready. A church in Seattle is its own social animal: This city leaves you be, whether you're sitting on a stool at the corner bar, browsing library stacks, or sliding into a pew. Introverts like me live here for a reason.

Newcomers

Grace was planted in Seattle by the Presbyterian Church of America, the PCA, a conservative arm of Presbyterianism established in the 1970s. Inspired by the work Tim Keller had been doing at Redeemer Presbyterian in New York City, Grace was founded in the late '90s to "love the city."

Drew and I visited Grace a few weeks after we moved to Seattle in 2004 and never left. We'd been told that several musicians we listened to had been spotted in the pews. And we felt at home when listening to sermons by John, the senior pastor. They were thoughtful and relevant to our lives as newcomers in the city. Instead of a praise band, there were strings and original hymn arrangements. I didn't know anything about the governance or structure of the PCA, but I knew I was drawn to this particular church. It was a place that welcomed heavy readers, professionals, creatives, and folks who felt more drawn to liturgy than charismatic call-and-response services.

Grace was a soft place to land in the early 2000s, especially if you were bookish and shy. There were two dynamics at play in those years—Drew's and my introversion and the church's disposition to let people engage when they were ready. Neither of those things were bad, per se, but our lukewarm engagement dragged on for too long. I needed that kind of church until I didn't; eventually, my anonymity became old news to me. I was increasingly lonely; the cohousing group we'd moved across the country to start disbanded after two years. We'd lost the ease of community that had been found most nights in our shared living room. I was ready to welcome new friendships at Grace. But I was ashamed that it had taken me so long to want to be included at church, so I stayed where I was comfortable, which was to be disengaged.

Finally, one winter I went to a Grace women's weekend at Rainbow Lodge, an '80s-style retreat center at the foothills of the Cascades. Asher was a babe in arms, still nursing, and I brought him along. I stood and rocked him in a baby carrier at the back of the room during sessions. I awkwardly changed him in the corners of the gathering space. I lugged his car seat to happy hour at a hotel overlooking a waterfall that a group of us drove to on a free afternoon. There was jammy pinot and overpriced flatbread topped with pear and gorgonzola.

At a small group breakout session at the lodge that night, the leader asked my name and how long I'd been coming to Grace. "I'm Sara, I've been coming for, eh, *eight* years?"

"Why haven't we seen you before?" she asked. I burned with embarrassment, then a deep sadness. Driving home that night near Snoqualmie Pass, I felt as anonymous as the Cascades you could barely see, just sense they were there. I was space and weight; I filled a chair in the breakout session circle. But I did not belong.

Still not deeply connected at Grace, we eventually considered leaving. You might be thinking, *What's wrong with them? Why did they stay for so long if they felt disconnected?* We stayed because though we weren't growing, we weren't shrinking in our faith either. On some level, I knew our quiet, observant dispositions would travel with us to another congregation.

The Benedictine vow of stability binds monks to a community. I suppose we were mirroring it, this vow of staying rooted, even if we didn't know it at the time. The water we were treading was warm. Sometimes, it was restorative, like a hot spring on the Olympic Peninsula. No one seems sure of the benefits of the minerals and steam, but maybe something unseen was happening, maybe some toxins were being released.

Wanting to Be Welcomed

I noticed during a recent trip to western Michigan that Christianity is all over the place. Christian radio is on every other station, not just the left end of the dial alternating with public radio. On one radio show, two women were talking about soil preparation for seed planting and peppering in language about God, the master gardener. A friend told me that if I looked around the room at any café in Grand Rapids, I could be guaranteed someone is reading the Bible. He did not say this sarcastically, just practically. Church is a part of the regional culture, like tulip festivals and soft serve at Captain Sundae.

The next day, I walked into a coffee roaster on the outskirts of Holland, Michigan, and saw a group of young people sitting around with their Bibles. Spotting me, the leader looked embarrassed, trailed off when saying, "The great thing about Jesus . . ." and took an intentional sip from his mug. I wondered if I looked like an atheist—if an atheist looked like a middle-aged white lady in wrinkled barrel pants and a sweatshirt. In retrospect, I probably just looked grumpy.

I felt annoyed and judgmental seeing so many manifestations of Christianity in western Michigan. After twenty years of living in Seattle, I had become used to the fact that there is no social capital to be gained by outward signs of faith in my city. To read a Bible in a café would be seen as performative or absurd.

Then I wondered what was wrong with me. Was I defensive and hardened, my reaction to the Bible study in the Michigan café a reflection of how I carry myself? I remembered the cold welcome I'd been given at Grace years before, and I wondered now whether it was because of my city, the makeup of the congregation in those days, or my standoffishness. The truth is there was a warmth in Michigan that I wouldn't let myself feel because I was suspicious that it was not genuine. I probably othered myself in the café to feel in control of my perceived outsiderness.

That choice separated me from others. "A Christian doctrine of creation is first a doctrine of place and people, of divine love and divine touch, of human presence and embrace and of divine and human interaction,"[1] writes Willie Jennings in *The Christian Imagination*. That sentence is convicting: God meets us through other people, but we must be willing to be met.

Where we live forms us, and it forms our churches. Travelers can sense welcome or the lack of it when they come to your town. When you travel, you probably notice whether you are made to feel at home or are received with suspicion. The trick for people like me is to not kick a gift horse in the mouth. The trick is to want to be welcomed.

Spirit-Led Moments

Last year, I visited a large church in Portland, Oregon, with my family and our friends. During worship, the people in front of us weren't just lifting a hand, they were raising both hands, pumping their arms. I was withering, self-aware but still wishing I was the kind of person who could worship with abandon. *The better Christian could do it*, I thought. They could put God over being embarrassed.

Leaning toward me, Asher whispered during the second song, "Mom, is something wrong with our church? Because we don't worship like this. I can kind of feel God's presence here more easily." After he said that, I began to pay closer attention to what was happening around us. There are always those of us in worship settings who are less inclined to raise our hands and who are more self-inhibited. Maybe we'll keep our elbows glued to our sides and cup our hands to the ceiling in a low tuck, a sort of military stance. Looking around, I saw other people in the crowd who looked like I must have, lightly swaying on the weight of our heels, heads slightly down, sort of mouthing the words.

As the service continued, I kept thinking about what my kid asked. Was our usual liturgy and solemn music—beautiful and aesthetically appealing—not breaking through to my teenage son? Was he gaining a restfulness in our liturgy and a focus on contemplation on Sunday at Grace but not given the eyes to look for Holy Spirit–led moments? Was he not finding those moments as often because of our church's style—or because of how I modeled worship back to him?

Years before, as a teen and twentysomething, I had tried to feel my way to God, but it hadn't worked. Anxious to avoid the need to see God move in order to believe in God, I stopped expecting God to show up in worship. And still, despite my doubts, it did happen at times. That clean feeling when the Holy Spirit manifests, the weighted calm I had experienced in life when I'd been open to it, is what I wanted for myself and my family. As a young adult, I would never have imagined that I would find it in monastic and Catholic practices. And yet I did.

Jennings says that "the right relationships . . . involve deep joining, the opening of lives to one another in love and desire."[2] A lot of us, including me, invest in the opposite of deep joining: individualism. Maybe we have cultivated a sense that we're not attached to a place, leaving home for the city or leaving the city for the suburbs. Sometimes we leave one place because we have to: we can't afford to buy a house, we need help from family with childcare, or we become a caregiver to a sick parent. Other times we leave because we are bored or unsatisfied, and we wonder if a new place can fix the roaming part of our heart looking for rest.

The same goes for church. After our visit to the congregation in Portland, I wondered again about our staying at the same church for twenty years. Did we eventually become rooted because we were faithful in following God's call to stay at Grace, or was it because we were comfortable? Jennings calls us to a theology infused with where we are, with its racial, class, and social dynamics. To be connected and invested for the long term in a fabric of relationships requires investing in a deep joining that is at times very uncomfortable. But it can also be holy work.

Really Singing

Drew and I moved further into the community at Grace in the 2010s when Debbie Smith Tacke joined the church's staff. Debbie became my first spiritual director and introduced our congregation to half-day silent retreats, Quaker clearness committees, lectio divina, and other contemplative practices. I learned to pray by listening first, rather than by rambling a list of the day's anxieties to God. I started using my imagination to interact with Jesus and to sit with verses about God's love. Debbie couldn't have come at a better time for me or our church. Our pastor John was applying more formative practices and growing personally in a way that shined in his sermons. We hired a new music director, Jess, who built on the legacy of Grace's strings and hymns and now leads with a present, earnest steadiness that disarms people. Nothing changed, except we kept showing up to the service each Sunday with whatever we were carrying.

"We bring bodies that fear failure, rejection, or being out of control. We bring bodies that are burdened by sickness and self-hatred. We bring disfigured and dispirited bodies," W. David O. Taylor writes about the gathered church. "We bring bodies that have been scarred by touch and bodies that have been starved of touch. And on account of the insidious effects of sin, we bring broken ways of relating to our own bodies and the bodies of others who gather with us in a common space of worship."[3] I began to see these very things at Grace: bodies that seemed to relax when we worked through the week's liturgy together.

This idea—that worship restores—would sound idealistic if we weren't all so clumsy, awkward, and tired, if a lot of us were less bothered by one affliction or another. "The church is a body, made up of many parts—arms, legs, eyes, ears, all learning to live and move harmoniously through life as one. Most churches most often resemble the body of a preteen, gangly, awkward, uncoordinated, and clumsy, to be sure; but such realities invite us to lean into, not away from, the timeless call to be embodied," Pastor Jay Kim says.[4] When God brings collective peace over a broken body of worshipers gathered together, it can be beautiful.

More people started to really sing for the first time at Grace, and sometimes I sensed that clean lightness of the Holy Spirit I'd missed. I felt more connected and drawn to the healthy staff and leadership dynamics. In the years that followed, I became a deacon and Drew became an elder.

A Choreography of Love

Like many churches, since the 2016 election, Grace has lost a lot of people and welcomed some new ones. We've tried to navigate a country-wide rise in Christian nationalism, a pandemic, and the Black Lives Matter movement in our local context. The building where Grace meets is located within walking distance of CHOP/CHAZ, the area in our Capitol Hill neighborhood declared self-autonomous by protestors near the east precinct of the Seattle police department in the summer of 2020. While the barricaded blocks were occupied, members of the congregation brought water bottles to the protestors, dropped off socks and toothbrushes, organized meals, and met with other local church leaders to pray.

After church one Sunday, Asher and I checked out the public art and community food tent at CHOP and saw a listening circle of people led by leaders of color. Then we went home and read news coverage declaring the space a manifestation of anarchy, such as a piece from the *New York Post*: "How the Seattle CHOP zone went from socialist summer camp to deadly disaster."[5] For our church, showing up as nonjudgmental presences offering practical care was the best way we knew to be steady when our city was on edge, kindled by misinformed media.

We're a church in the city, and our city like other cities is trying, failing, and trying again to navigate the opioid epidemic, provide housing for the unhoused, and protect vulnerable people from hate crimes. Grace has made it a practice to look around the community for examples of practical love that extend beyond church doors. Just as all creation and beauty is breathed by God, we've learned that God's love often comes through other people. Said simply, God made everyone, God loves everyone, and God brings humanity and care to the world through each of us.

Sometimes, that love is most powerfully observed in the stories of fellow citizens such as Joël Barraquiel Tan, then executive director of the Wing Luke Museum in Seattle's Chinatown-International District. Tan referenced the rise in racism toward Asian Americans in an interview on our local NPR station. In September of 2023, a hate crime was committed by a man swinging a sledgehammer and busting the glass at the Wing Luke the same night as a nearby Beyoncé concert.[6]

In the interview, Tan talked about what he calls a "choreography of love" that emerged directly after the incident. Many people, some walking past and dressed for the concert and others inside the museum, sprang to action—calling for help, calling the mayor's office, grabbing brooms and sweeping up. Love in practice through tangible care.

For days after I heard the interview, my mind kept coming back to the idea of a choreography of love. I wondered if the church could still move like that.

Regardless of whether someone was religious, the general public used to view the church in America as a positive part of society. The church was seen as a helper, like a librarian or a firefighter. However, the church's position relative to society started gradually shifting in the late 1900s, speeding up in the 2000s when news about sex abuse scandals broke in the Catholic church that roiled throughout the entire church.

Help is no longer the driving narrative of the church. We know about hypocrisy in the church whether we like it or not, whether we believe in God or not, if we read the news. Faithful local congregations serving quietly generally aren't newsworthy. Imagine a headline less interesting than this: "Baptist Church Organizes Holiday Food Drive."

Stability in the world also feels more and more like a thing of the past, and the church is struggling to keep up. Whatever your opinion on social issues, including abortion, gender, sexuality, and politics, any culture war narrative moves faster than institutions do. If a denomination changes its stance on women clergy, for example, it doesn't change overnight. Anchored in the past, denominations tend to shift over decades, not months or even years. There's a dissonance between the pace of polity and the speed at which information shifts and voracious digital consumption sparks behavior change in culture. Even if a church doesn't want to seem clunky, it often does, like a university or corporation.

Then there's performative change, which is little better for a church than the silence that often messages complicity. Countless organizations and businesses issued a Black Lives Matter statement after the murder of George Floyd in 2020, whether or not they were instituting genuine DEI training and practices. And if they didn't, a statement's absence was discussed and politicized. Requisite but hollow messages of support are not what the church needs if we're trying to quell anxiety.

Instead, paradoxically, most work of discernment paced with the gospel is probably going to be out of time with the cadence of social change, which can cause even the wisest and most earnest church to appear irrelevant or avoidant. The best way to tell the difference between silence that is political and silence that is discerning is to participate in the conversation.

Captured Hearts

Like any group of people, on a given Sunday our congregation is filled with people whose hearts are all over the place. Strengthened, afraid, peaceful, angry. We welcome people to come with whatever they are carrying, to hang back if they want to until they are ready to engage. Liturgy helps to unify us, calls us to stillness, and never nudges performative worship because it draws us inward first and then meets us collectively.

I heard mentor and friend Winn Collier talk about why pastors are burned out and why this anxious church era has so many hurdles for clergy like him. "Where I immediately go is the fracture in our own hearts," he said. "I'm not sure that our current theological arrangements, our ecclesial way of going about things, or much anything about our current life actually fosters in us a deep and abiding sense of God's ongoing transformation."[7] What does? Beauty.

A generative belief in Jesus that shapes how we live and act in the world is rarely the result of the coaxing of someone who presents faith like a product. For pastors, the compulsion to share the beauty and joy of God can sound like a sales pitch. Even if it comes from a place of good intention or meaning, the posture of one person selling a message and the other person being sold is obvious. No one I've known has moved into belief in Christ in this way. No one in the pews answered altar calls in my youth in a tent revival–style call-and-response. Whatever growth model may have worked for Billy Graham stopped resonating a long time ago in the broader American church.

"I think many of us are trying, with good intentions, to cajole other people into a way of life that hasn't really captured our heart yet," Collier said.[8] In addition to cultivating beauty, how does the church bear a peaceful presence? By raising pastors who model commitment, empathy, and forgiveness before telling anyone else to. The personal work of leaders to bear calm and peace as news breaks, as people suffer, and as communities fail rolls down to congregants and calls everyone to loving action.

If God made the church, let God grow it. That's God's job. It's the church's job to model humility and to mend when harm is perpetuated. A healthy church will welcome people and send them off well. Its people will keep breaking each other's hearts, forgiving each other when we're able, and navigating individual grief and systemic anxiety. A healthy church will show up for one another—a family who needs groceries, parents advocating for education for a neurodivergent child, a student struggling with addiction.

A healthy church will be stable, constant, and intentionally make space for the lonely, anxious woman who sits in the back most Sundays to move toward the welcome on offer when she is ready.

10

Fidelity

I imagine how the church might look without anxiety: a forest floor sanctuary covered in pine needles, the air fresh and sweet from mint, forest animals asleep within a circle of trees. Then I snap out of it. Far from a woodland refuge that offers relief from anxiety, the American church in our time is tense from both inside and outside forces.

It is either supremely naive (as imaginary as an alfresco pine tree sanctuary) to believe Christians can practice faithfulness to each other across ideological divides, or it's a prerequisite for moving forward in an anxious age.

Once again, I looked to the Benedictines for relief and found inspiration for what faithfulness in action looks like through their vow of fidelity. The Latin term *conversatio morum* is from the Rule of St. Benedict and is generally defined as a long-term commitment to monasticism.[1]

Benedictine fidelity shows us what commitment to a way of being—and to one another—looks like in practice. The

Sisters of St. Benedict in southern Indiana describe the Benedictine fidelity in their monastery in a grounded way: "This vow allows us to rub the rough edges from ourselves and each other. It helps us to say that we choose to be faithful to this way of life, in the good and bad times. In the time of finding the pearl of great price and the time of losing it. . . . We are working toward the buried treasure of monastic life together."[2] If stability allows us to be present and long-suffering, fidelity keeps us faithful to God and each other while moving toward a common purpose. This work deepens by extending grace to people across the pew and especially those who hold different and uncomfortable ideologies on social issues including gender, sexuality, and women in leadership.

A Theology for Our Time

Speaking about cultural systems in her 2016 lecture, "A Theology for the Moment," Marilynne Robinson acknowledges that loving our enemy requires acknowledging our differences, "which would surely mean taking on that most difficult and humbling realization, that what they intend for evil, God, in the course of historic time, might well intend for good."[3]

Robinson continues to explain how a theology that "would embrace rather than exclude would be a departure, not only from its own troublesome history but from the narrowness and aridity of the secular thinking that has displaced it."[4] Maybe you read Robinson's words and smiled. Because she has just said, in a sentence, the thing you might sense at your gut level: Instead of being an anxious Christian working to protect the status quo because it's familiar, one can be a Christian that moves closer to God's goodness through embracing expansiveness.

You might also have read Robinson's call for inclusion with a check in your gut. Is a "theology for our time" a watered-down bourbon when you want a straight shot? Is a call for expansiveness a literary way of articulating a slippery slope? Is Robinson's theology appeasing and essentially saying nothing?

Personally, I find Robinson's words to be a relief for anyone wanting to pursue serious practice with open palms. Robinson goes on to define "a theology for our time" as one that "could create a conceptual space large enough to accommodate human dignity."[5] Here, she is especially concerned with how we lovingly live together in an ideologically diverse world, bearing faithfulness that honors creation. This calm energy works against anxiety.

In a broad sense, conservatives are anxious because culture is changing at lightning speed, and the church's influence in American society is shrinking; one could argue the anxiety of these Christians is contributing to the church's failings. Progressives are anxious because the church is not responding quickly enough, is not malleable, and is increasingly irrelevant. And churches "in the middle" are anxious because they're accused of being lukewarm, not taking a clear stance, and they're working to be faithful in the swirl of change, seeing and sensing the tensions from all sides.

I suspect that those of us trying to practice Christianity by focusing on the way of Jesus while being pulled to fully embrace the left or right suffer from high anxiety because we have no relief. We have no camp; we're not connected or organized. And if we became organized, we'd probably become another faction that separates instead of unifies. It makes me wonder, When we gain belonging, do we risk losing a spiritual posture that welcomes across differences? In an era when ideating about reaching a middle ground is labeled as colonialist and privileged, even talking about loving our neighbor can be labeled as naive and suppressed supremacy. Either side can use us as an example of fodder to fuel their own position. It is easier to be quiet. The problem is, not speaking up does not quell anxiety; it grows it.

What then is the alternative if we're seeking something different? How do we learn to live in a way that is consistent with conviction and steeped in love? We get broader; we include instead of exclude. We read Robinson and relax.

In *Exclusion and Embrace*, Miroslav Volf offers a practical reason to build connection by absorbing pain and relinquishing the right to retribution and revenge. Volf is from the former Yugoslavia, where his family was impacted by ethnic cleansing as Serbians slaughtered Muslims. There is a vitality to Volf's call to unity: It is a matter of life or death. *God, if Volf can embrace unity, help all of us to do so too.*[6]

We're All Broken

Working across denominations and traditions, the British theologian Lesslie Newbigin calls Protestant, Pentecostal, and Catholic Christians together in his seminal 1953 writing on ecclesiology, *The Household of God*. Newbigin starts by stating the obvious: We're all broken.

He writes, "The ultimate problem of the Church, the seat of the perplexity which surrounds all systematic thought about it, is that it is at once holy and sinful."[7] Church anxiety lives in that dissonance. "The Church itself is the visible company of those who have been called by Him into the fellowship of his Son."[8] The lesson here, for our time and place in American Christianity, is clear: Broaden our borders so we can take our faith seriously. Learn how to love without certainty of right and wrong for the sake of the other.

The church isn't supposed to be a place we only go to for comfort. It's a place we also go to expecting we'll be wounded—but also persisting, like Jennings, for the long story. Kathleen Norris writes about the church in *Amazing Grace*:

> The church is like the Incarnation itself, a shaky proposition. It is a human institution, full of ordinary people, sinners like me, who say and do cruel, stupid things. But it is also a divinely inspired institution, full of good purpose, which partakes of a unity far greater than the sum of its parts. That is why it is called the body of Christ. And that is why, when the battles rage, people hold on. They find a sufficient unity, and a rubbed raw but sufficient love, and even the presence of God.[9]

We can't excuse abuse, violence, or hate. But we *can* learn how to love when it's uncomfortable. Doing so makes us more human and lets us see "the other" as a brother or sister. Or maybe more like a sibling, with the kind of tension and love that only comes through a shared experience of family.

Fathers and Brothers

Grace used to be Presbyterian, and now we are Anglican. Anglicanism is just as broken as any other tradition, being made up of broken people. We joined the Anglican Church with eyes open. We discerned together for a year. We took our time.

We as a church changed denominations after years of congregations, including ours, facing discipline over the role of women in leadership in the PCA. In our case, we were reprimanded for allowing women to be deacons, a practice that the regional presbytery had previously permitted. Years later, after complaints from leaders in other churches, our exception was threatened to be reversed.

In the fall of 2021, there was a large regional presbytery meeting in which the matter of Grace's women deacons would be discussed and voted on by pastors from across Washington State, Oregon, Idaho, and Alaska. Drew and I attended the meeting at a church on the east side of Seattle along with three or four other women in leadership at Grace.

There is a common language at presbytery meetings. At the beginning of each comment, the male speaker addresses the group with the salutation, "fathers and brothers." I sat in the room for hours, listening to remarks on various issues, with pastors using the salutation dozens of times. *Fathers and brothers. Fathers and brothers.* Being visible but unseen was surreal.

Near the end of the meeting, Grace's charges were presented. Men spoke for and against our deacon policy for about an hour. There was time for one more comment, which Drew, then an elder at Grace, delivered. He walked to the front of the room and said, "I would like to start by addressing our sisters of Christ in the room, who are colaborers with us in our work of God's kingdom." My body relaxed. I was seen, recognized, for the first time all afternoon, and it was by my husband. In that moment, I saw Drew in a new way. He is an educator and a confident speaker. But I had not seen him command a room or speak with such conviction before. He was, in that moment, wonderfully pastoral. You could have heard a pin drop.

The vote went our way, women could stay deacons. I felt like a woman in a Western gold rush town who was now allowed to show her ankles under her prairie skirt. Still, I wondered what I was doing in the PCA. Why had we never looked into the denomination when joining Grace or seriously considered the matter of women in leadership before?

After the vote, pastors from the regional presbytery wrote letters refuting the decision, and it was eventually reversed. Grace was given a short time frame to remove women from the diaconate. Our church voted to leave the PCA a few months later. Drew and I joined Grace in 2004 because we liked the church. More than a decade later, as we moved into lay leadership roles in the congregation, we became enmeshed in the larger denomination's politicized posturing to protect the status quo. This doubling down against women in leadership roles was a reflection of the PCA's larger shift toward becoming more conservative that was mirrored in other denominations across the US.

Can women preach? For many of the men in that room or in any convention or meeting debating church polity, this question is not about the actual call of women. Whether complementarian or egalitarian, the discussion is often not about women's gifts to lead and pastor. It is political. The doubling down is driven by a perceived sense by these church leaders that America is becoming a less safe place to be a Christian than it used to be. The media is the enemy, Hollywood is the enemy, the gay and trans community is the enemy, and Democrats are the enemy. Instead of adopting Jennings's call to "divine and human interaction" or Robinson's call to expansiveness, these pastors band together. I wonder if, at least before the 2024 election, they were afraid of becoming irrelevant, or if they worried that in the broader culture they already were. The anxiety of that stance—that your way of being in the world is threatened—leads to defensiveness.

After exploring several denominations, the church voted to leave the PCA and join the Church for the Sake of Others (C4SO) diocese of the Anglican Church of North America. This process of exploring where we might find a denominational home unified the leadership team and helped us solidify our identity. During the pandemic when there was less and less unity to be found in larger culture, the year of discernment around the future of our church was refreshing. A few folks in the congregation voted to stay in the PCA, mostly in the hope we could work to change the Book of Church Order, the PCA's constitution that contains documentation of governance. I said in a meeting before the vote that we could stay and try, but the staff and lay leaders were very tired, and we simply wanted margin to focus on our people and our community. One man left as a result of the vote, and eventually, a few families followed. But overall, there was a building momentum, a sense that we were moving ahead and staying true to what God was doing at Grace.

After joining the C4SO, where women preach in many congregations, there was no choice but to do the work around the question of women's leadership. We spent a year reading, praying, discussing, and discerning women in leadership as a vestry and church. Putting his seminary degree to use, Drew joined Grace's staff the next year and began the ordination process for becoming a priest alongside John and others, including Jamie, who was ordained as our first female priest. Jamie had joined to lead Grace's community formation work just before the pandemic. A graduate of the PCA's Covenant Seminary, she never thought preaching was on the table. It was profound to see the call to preaching and pastoring grow in her and for her to be joyfully received by the church when she was ordained. A bunch of us took photos after the ceremony and ate fried chicken in the fellowship hall.

John told Jamie in front of the church that her being ordained wasn't about her or Grace only but more precisely about the generosity of God "so that the church may be built up" in its work (1 Cor. 14:26). When watching her preach for the first time, I said to Sabine, "Look! It's Jamie!" I was proud to experience the moment with my daughter, for her to see herself reflected from the pulpit. My kid shrugged. "*Of course*, Jamie is preaching, Mom," she said. "Why wouldn't she be?"

There is sweetness in remaining a part of a community that changes, and it requires bearing faithfulness through loss. I'm not sure it does a lot of good to be in relationship with others when life is going well if we don't know how to hold one another's afflictions. I looked around at Grace one Sunday and thought, *We're tired but we're healthy*. I remembered St. Thérèse's daily offering, in which she prays for the grace to "accept for love of [God] the joys and sorrows of this passing life." We had done that, together. Almost twenty years later, through joy and sorrow, I was more fully known by people I hadn't chosen.

"I'll Carry This with You"

One Sunday, Jamie asked the congregation to stand in a circle around the sanctuary. She held two large rocks and passed one to the person on her left and the other to the person on her right. "Take the rock, and if you feel safe in doing so, tell the person next to you one or two things you're carrying," Jamie explained. The person next to you can say, "By the grace of God I'll carry this with you." I looked around the room and saw an intimacy and trust that was hard-won. I passed the rock to Asher after it came to me. He told me what he was carrying, and we both started to cry. "By the grace of God, Asher, I'll carry this with you." It was my honor to do so both as his mother and as a member of his church community. It wasn't the same kind of experiential moment we'd felt at the church in Portland. But in that moment, God showed up.

Therapist Chuck DeGroat writes:

> Where trust is low and anxiety is high within a church or Christian org, I don't care how loudly you proclaim the name of Jesus or how well you cast vision, you will find it hard to avoid the constant drumbeat of drama, division, discontent and dysfunction. The reality is—highly anxious systems don't thrive. Within them, creativity is stifled and connection is eroded. No amount of vision-casting or mission-articulating, no repetition of praise songs, no amount of incentivizing and motivating, will tame the beast of anxiety.[10]

DeGroat is right. When we're anxious together, we can't perform or vision cast our way out. He continues, "Only the hard work of fostering trust and authentic connection, honest self-assessment and deep confession, real safety and equal accountability, and a shared vision that emerges from the collective creativity that trust breeds can begin to shift a system from anxiety to trust."[11] In other words, we have to stick together and listen to each other. We have to be willing to change and bear each other's burdens.

Die Tired

I listened to peers defend doctoral projects at the end of a DMin program I completed at the Eugene Peterson Center for the Christian Imagination in the spring of 2024. A good handful of the cohort were pastor-writers in the path of Peterson, who was both. After a presentation on the vulnerability of leading a church of people, the questions turned confessional in a way that I felt moving. "As clergy, this work will cost you everything," one peer said. It will wear you down. "I want to die tired," my friend Daniel said. At this, I thought of Drew.

I sometimes wonder why God calls us at certain times. Why now, at midlife, was Drew becoming a priest? The twist of entering ministry in middle age is that you are already tired. In Drew's case, there's also a benefit to becoming a priest in your forties—you have seen a thing or two. In some ways, he and I are just kids. We have no idea how much we will lose or how foolish we are for trying. If you start late with your eyes open, are you wise or doubly foolish?

Shortly after Drew was hired at Grace and he began the process of becoming ordained, I realized I would become a priest's wife. I wondered how I should show up now that we sat more toward the front of the sanctuary. I was well past my "we've never seen you before" era and knew most of the folks at Grace by their first names. I'd slowly grown to love our church and to find a sense of belonging.

I considered buying long floral dresses. I considered asking the kids to brush their hair before the service and worried that the dreaded "pastor's kid" designation would pressure them to show up one way on Sunday but live another until they couldn't handle the dissonance and went wild. Then I remembered Grace. I remembered my specific church and these specific people. I set down the pastor's wife persona before I tried it on. I'd show up as me in '90s mom jeans and vintage T-shirts, and if that was good enough for God, it was enough for Grace.

Warm Loaves

When we open ourselves to the love of God instead of trying to act like a false version of ourselves, we change. But being honest also means we open ourselves up to vulnerability and suffering. It's like that with people, and it's like that in church.

Newbigin writes tenderly about the church, but he doesn't skim over what the church loses in order to be found: "Her life is to be forever spent, to be cast into the ground like a corn of wheat, in the ever-new faith and hope of the resurrection harvest."[12] My mother was young, and she peeled the kernel out of each piece of popped corn. I was a child, and I grew up. There was relative political discourse, and now there is political chaos. The church grows, sprouts, and splits like we do, in seasons and cycles.

The church calms down by practicing fidelity. The church calms down by doing work with our hands. The church quells anxiety by looking to our left and right. Living small, showing up, bandaging wounds alongside beleaguered people. A gardener has to break up solid ground before something new is seeded. Maybe it matters more that we did the planting and less that we're here to see the sowing, the baking, and the slicing of a warm loaf at the table.

11

Energy Vampires

The New York Times ran a 6-Day Energy Challenge in January of 2024. Daily themes were on topics like how to eat better and gain more focus. Day four stuck out to me: Identify your "energy vampires" and "chaotic friends." The article invites readers to conduct a "friendship audit"[1] and lists questions to consider to determine if a person in your life is an energy vampire:

- Who, if anyone, do you consistently put off seeing or dread responding to?
- Who often makes you feel so irritated, keyed up, or fatigued that you have to recover after seeing them?
- Who makes you regularly zone out during conversations because they aren't involving you?[2]

Oprah was interviewed for the article and said, "You are with the wrong friend 'if you are around anybody that makes you feel less than 100 percent yourself, if you're around anybody that makes you feel like you can't shine or say whatever you want to say.'"[3]

I'm certain I've been an "energy vampire" to friends in different times, and I can think of a few people in my life who would fit the bill of those three questions—friends who feed my anxiety. But I winced when I read this article. The message underneath a vampire friend audit is clear: We can dictate who is in our lives based on how they make us feel; we need to be close to people who can do something for us. I wasn't comfortable with that.

Don't get me wrong: No one should be forced to stay in a relationship or a church that is abusive or remain in any setting where harm is done. But consumerism is dripping all over the notion of the friendship audit. I can freshen up friends like a wardrobe. The same thinking can apply to a church that isn't perfect—which is every church.

I thought about the article for several days and reread it a few times. I wondered if my frequent emotional hangovers were a sign of some internal draining, a drawing out of my personal stores of energy. Psychiatrist Judith Orloff explains that emotional hangovers are "'energetic residue' left over from an interaction with an 'energy vampire,' or someone who, intentionally or not, saps your mental and emotional energy."[4] *Ha*, I thought. Sure, other people can deplete us. But what do you do when you suck the life out of yourself? What do you do when you are, in fact, your own energy vampire?

I began the Ignatian Exercises in 2023 around the same time I was thinking about energy vampires. I had some personal work to do in understanding how we can be our own worst enemy. Part of the nine-month retreat (for me, an hour in the morning before work) involves asking God to surface our authentic and false selves so that we can begin to differentiate our appetites from God's desire for our lives. The authentic self is rooted in God's love. The parts of us driven by love reveal our true identity. I have mine and you have yours.

Thomas Merton wrote in *New Seeds of Contemplation*, "My false and private self is the one who wants to exist outside the reach of God's will and God's love."[5] My "false self" surfaced quickly over the first weeks of the retreat, featuring emotional heavy hitters such as loneliness and ego. My authentic self surfaced in gentler ways, including an inclination toward faithfulness.

Loneliness diminishes when we're committed to a group of people. Unfortunately, the ego can be poked and feelings hurt. When we pursue a part of our authentic self, which in my case involves a bent toward fidelity, that desire is usually tested. Church is a petri dish.

I want to be in a community with people I can learn from even if we don't have the same taste or a lot in common. I want to grow to love people who are not like me, those younger and older than me with different stories and experiences. I believe that's what a healthy church community looks like. That's how empathy grows. But first and always, new and uncomfortable interpersonal situations pop up; there are constant invitations to choose kindness, patience, and self-control.

Relational Faithfulness

Jesus once said that the one without sin could cast the first stone. If we cultivate a world where we cut loose anyone who drags us down, we're projecting a message to others in our life that we might cut them off too. And we're introducing relational instability in our own life, knowing we also could be cut loose in a time of need.

Instead, relational faithfulness cultivates the radical and enduring acceptance we all long for—in both good and bad seasons. Centering faithfulness in relationships is a better way forward. And there are better questions for any "friend audits" we might conduct:

- Are my friend and I practicing mutuality and giving each other the benefit of the doubt?
- Is my friend bringing me toward my authentic self and helping me to see myself as loved?
- Do we want to see each other flourish?
- Does this relationship help me reach across difference and grow in empathy?

We can ask similar questions about a church:

- Does this church center power on one leader or make room for many voices, including my own?
- Do we grapple with or shy away from difficult questions and differences in community?
- Do I see life here, a pouring out into the community?
- Is this a place where people can hold healthy tension across the aisle on political and social issues?

Questions like these are not motivated by a need to edit or limit exposure to discomfort and potentially difficult conversations. These questions may require confronting anxiety about how a relationship can or should change. But instead of asking us to react based on feelings, they can support a healthy discernment process around our commitments with friendships or church.

No Contact

In *Monsters*, Claire Dederer explores the question, What do we do with good art created by "bad people"? People such as Roman Polanski, Woody Allen, Kanye. How can and should we consume work when its creator is complicated, broken, and in some cases predatory? Does reckoning with their bad behavior mean that we have to leave their art behind?

In an interview on Vox's *Gray Area* podcast, Dederer talks to host Constance Grady about how "no contact culture" is showing up more often on social feeds and in therapy sessions. "We're living in this moment where it's kind of trendy in advice columns, Reddit, TikTok and other places for people to advise other people to just cut off contact with someone when they're terrible and just cut them out of your life," Grady says. "There are certainly times when that is the move to make."[6]

It's true. Some relationships are toxic and should shift or end for our health or safety. But as an idea, going "no contact" dovetails nicely with a "friendship audit" in a wellness challenge. Both cloak the myth that we can relationally curate ourselves into being a better version of ourselves as a self-care practice. But we can't self-create our way into being a healthy friend. We have to do the work, and to start we have some fessing up to do.

"People are terrible. We all have terrible parts of ourselves," Dederer says. "Pointing the finger at the other guy and saying 'you're terrible' is the easy thing to do. But the fact is, we all have dark parts of ourselves. And it's not just 'How do I get along with this family member who's been rotten to me?' But turning it around and remembering maybe sometimes I am that family member."[7]

Drew and I listened to this conversation on a road trip and were buzzing with thoughts after. Dederer, coming from a secular framework, is essentially dealing with sin and the fact that all people are broken. We may see big figures crash and burn, but she's essentially saying we all live with preemptive shame: *What if the gaze is turned on me? What if I'm told I am a monster?*

There is a collective anxiety about exposure because we all have something we'd rather hide. That dovetails with the Christian story: Everyone will "fall short of the glory of God" (Rom. 3:23). And like Dederer, we can arrive at a place of empathy for everyone because we're all broken.

Many years ago, Kathleen Norris met with her pastor after receiving the dubious assignment of teaching a women's Bible study on the book of Revelation. This was the mid-'90s, when, "in our own century, the Antichrist has been equated to Adolf Hitler, Joseph Stalin, Pol Pot, and given the current state of political hysteria in America, no doubt Bill and Hillary Clinton." Norris continues, "What the pastor said was so simple that it will remain with me forever. 'Each one of us acts as an

Antichrist . . . whenever we hear the gospel and do not do it.'"[8] Christians could swap "Antichrist" with "monster." The secular-sacred line blurs, and we're all one busted-up people who can only pray, *Help*.

What do we do when the monsters are pastors? For some of us, living in a no-contact culture means we don't want to touch church. Church has become the unclean thing. Church has become the thing that defiles.

We don't want to become unclean by handling anything taboo. If church is broken—which, let's be honest, it is—and I engage in it, does that grossness somehow transfer to my reputation? What does it say about who I am if I go to church? Is there a sort of guilt and shame laid on me just by association? Yes, in many cases this is how Christians are perceived, usually (and tragically) by other Christians who hold different political views. But somehow this exposure to the loss of reputation—that the practicing Christian is seen as an idealogue, a self-soother afraid of death, an anti-intellectual, or whatever—becomes irrelevant in the conviction of a life spent pursuing the upside-down kingdom of Jesus.

When healthy, the Christian life makes room for the care of the very ones who are rejected. There is justice and faithfulness, care for the vampiric, for all the monsters on all sides of the aisle. Maybe even care for ourselves.

12

Religious but Not Spiritual

I graduated with an English degree from a Christian liberal arts college in 2000. I drove to Manhattan a week later to begin NYU's Summer Publishing Institute. As a creative writing major and the editor of my campus literary magazine, I was thrilled by the idea of starting my career at an independent press. I planned to stay in the city and get a job in publishing after the program.

That summer, one of the young women in my Union Square dorm asked if she could borrow a CD. I fumbled through my collection and handed her Moby's 1999 *Play*. That album was released in an era when Moby was talking about Christianity, and there was a general sense from fans that Moby's stated love for Christ was a personality quirk, like his veganism. But to me, it was a hopeful example of the wide world accepting, even loving, a creative person while tolerating their faith.

Unfolding the *Play* CD sleeve, I read it aloud in a way that I hoped was casual. I wanted credibility and secretly felt pressure to witness to my dormmate. "Oh wow, I see that Moby writes about his faith," I said and shrugged. "It's cool because he talks about how 'the central tenets of the teachings of Christ are nonjudgmentalism, nonviolence, and humility.' I really relate to that." She raised an eyebrow, said "Thaaaaanks?" took the CD, and closed her bedroom door.

In those years, I was especially anxious about how my Christian faith would be received or rejected because I was embarrassed by it. So whenever I heard a well-known person mention Jesus, I paid special attention. Any public association was evidence that I could be creative, intellectual, and a Christian. Maybe I could get a pass like Moby. I was looking for someone else to legitimize my convictions because it was more important for me to be received than to be defined by a belief system steeped in cultural stereotypes I could not control.

Fast-forward from 2000 to 2018 when I decided to write publicly about my Christian identity. I say "publicly" because my website and social media profiles were no longer set to private. A small number of people read what I wrote, but I still had to scrape up the courage to get over myself first. No one cared about my faith identity like I did.

My writing was met with some skepticism but mostly grace and curiosity by people who read what I wrote and did not share my faith tradition. It was an immense relief. Ironically, some people in the bounds of the church were most critical of ideas they deemed to be too political. Some friends stopped reading my writing, wanting to avoid more evidence that I was walking perilously close to the edge of faith that would, in their minds, only be confirmed with another Instagram post about Christian nationalism.

Eighteen years after that Moby summer in my NYU dorm, Fleming Rutledge, one of the first women to become an ordained Episcopal priest in the 1970s, preached her Good Friday sermons up Fifth Avenue at St. Thomas Church, using words that reminded me of my earlier tensions and made me think about them in a new way. "There are elements of myself that are indefensible. There are elements of yourself that are indefensible," she said. "If you don't know that, you don't understand the grace of God."[1] I read this and thought, *There is no way for a person to defend hiding who you are or what you believe.* And there are a lot of good reasons to hide. Maybe it's no one's business what you believe. Maybe it's too much work to talk about why you're a Christian. Maybe your family would flip out if you talked about what your faith looks like, and the dissonance of your own life with theirs would be too much to hold.

But when we do not talk about belief, we miss the chance to receive grace from other people and move more fully into ourselves. If someone cares about you, they will probably want to understand why faith is important in your life—and that may be reason enough to try.

Oh, Beautiful World

In our current era, when the Western church is flailing and those of us left in it are carrying around low-grade anxiety about where we go from here, I continue to be curious about the ways Christianity is woven into broader cultural conversations. I had dinner with my friend Josh in Austin a couple of years ago. He'd recently become confirmed as a member of the Eastern Orthodox church and was talking about the beauty of iconography and the new congregation he attends. I talked about Anglicanism, our church's journey to changing denominations, and the steadiness of liturgy.

I thought about something Josh shared for weeks after we met. He'd been paying attention to observations from creative people who are drawn to Christ but who would not necessarily identify as Christian. "Take the Irish author Sally Rooney," he said.

Rooney's 2021 book, *Beautiful World, Where Are You*, includes letters between two friends, Alice and Eileen. Per usual with Rooney's novels, there is an expected amount of Millennial disillusionment and plenty of sex. But the friends also write about Christianity in a way that reads new and even pure—for example, this letter to Eileen from Alice:

> This morning, tired and disoriented, I wandered down the street near my hotel and eventually found and entered an empty church. There I sat for about twenty minutes bathed in the slow serious air of sanctity and cried a few picturesque tears about the nobility of Jesus. This is all by way of explaining to you my interest in Christianity—put simply, I am fascinated and touched by the "personality" of Jesus, in rather a sentimental, arguably even maudlin way. Everything about his life moves me. . . . He seems to me to embody a kind of moral beauty, and my admiration for that beauty even makes me want to say that I "love" him, though I'm well aware how ridiculous that sounds.[2]

Alice is not convinced of the divinity of Jesus; the book does not document a traditional conversion. But she experiences an interior shift, an open posture of curiosity that is not ironic or steeped in any family-of-origin trauma. She has no personal history with the church to recover from and is free to pursue Jesus.

As I read this passage, part of me was jealous of the character Alice. I wondered what it would feel like to discover Jesus now, to have skipped the end-times fear and culture war rhetoric of my childhood and young adulthood. Would coming to Christ late, well into adulthood, have meant I'd have a traceable before and after version of myself? Would the "after Sara" have been less anxious?

Prophetic Voices

Christian or not, literature, art, and music can be a form of worship if God is the author of all people and all of creation. This means writers, artists, and musicians can imperfectly, but profoundly, fill the job vacancy of prophet. Like a prophet, it's the role of the artist to offer incisive critique. And if there are few biblical prophets to be found these days, there are plenty of aesthetically-driven examples.

When we lean in and listen, clarity about the church can come from voices not steeped in Christianity. There is sometimes a real, charged presence in these voices. I had to listen to Nick Cave's *On Being* conversation with Krista Tippett in fifteen-minute chunks because there was much of Plato's three transcendentals—truth, goodness, and beauty—in what Cave said. He had been making the podcast rounds promoting the book *Faith, Hope and Carnage*, which he co-published with Irish journalist Seán O'Hagan.

Cave has lost two sons. He has moved through times of addiction and other desolations. But instead of balking at the idea of a higher power like some of his peers, Cave talked in the interview about how he is particularly drawn to Christ and attends church.

When asked about the reality of God, Cave says:

> It's extraordinarily difficult to argue your corner about these sorts of things against so-called rational, empirical truths about things. They have all the big guns. . . . I prefer to use the word religious rather than spiritual myself. . . . I've actually found a church in the UK. . . . The singing is so beautiful. The music, the organ player's off the charts. . . . It blows away my basic skeptical nature in a heartbeat. . . . By the time it gets to the communion, it's unbelievably moving, this service. In fact, this church has got a reputation of being the church for atheists because it's so beautiful that anyone can just feel these sorts of things.[3]

Tippett goes on to talk about the common phrase "spiritual, but not religious." She says, "Something that I think is also coming back is 'religious, but not spiritual.'"[4]

After listening to the interview, I turned the idea of "religious but not spiritual" around for a few days. Many people raised within evangelicalism were taught that Christianity is not just a religion. I was told as a kid that Christianity is a faith, a belief. Other religious traditions (Catholics were often thrown into the mix) were discredited as rituals or cultural curiosities. The sentiment was that "spiritual" implies faith and "religious" implies works, that you have to earn your way to redemption.

I've carried a negative view of the word "religion" into my adult life, as in, "Do not say my religion is Christianity." Even now, the word does not capture the breadth of faith for me. There is little *feeling* in it. Faith, of course, is not rooted in how we feel in a particular moment. But when I was growing up, faith was mainly expressed through people's emotions, visible in the pews—if I saw it at all.

Serious About Faith

I decided a few years ago that I wanted to become more serious about my Christian practice. I didn't want to waste my time going on about faith or writing about things I didn't believe to leverage book deals.

After that realization, I began to see a space for those within the Christian tradition—whether we are grappling with faith, questioning or doubting it, or approaching it with joy and grounded hope—to take the pursuit with the seriousness it deserves. To do this honors the Christian tradition—and dignifies its followers.

Within that context, the idea of "religious but not spiritual" began to make sense. I am a religious person. By that I mean I am a person serious about faith. That does not mean I do not struggle and doubt. It means, simply, that I am committed to Christianity and trying to let myself be known by God and formed by Jesus.

In practical terms, being religious means that I have embraced tested structures to help me grow. I try to pray the Daily Office. I attend a church that I've found to be safe and nurturing, and I meet with a spiritual director. This is what I do; it may or may not be what you do. I'm not interested in passing judgment on or providing a prescription for your practice or absence of practice. I am simply being honest about mine.

At one point in their *On Being* conversation, Tippett and Cave express their distaste for the word "spiritual." Eugene Peterson avoided it too. Peterson was inconsistent in its usage—after all, he held the title James M. Houston Professor of Spiritual Theology at Regent College. But I've talked to Peterson Center director, Winn Collier, about how Eugene largely skirted using the word "spiritual" as a descriptor. Essentially, as embodied people, we're all spiritual all the time, regardless of what we believe.

Peterson talked about his feelings about the word "spiritual" with Tippett in a 2016 *On Being* interview. "I think it's cheap," Peterson said. "You're taking something, putting a name on it, 'spiritual,' which means it's defined. The whole world is spiritual, and the word 'spirit' is 'wind,' it's 'breath.' Well, people are breathing all over the place; they're all spiritual beings, but if you have a name for it, you can compartmentalize it, and that just wreaks havoc with the whole thing."[5]

If you poke a few holes, it's easy to see how "religious but not spiritual" is a bit of a troubled phrase. These are not binaries, and again as spiritual beings, we're spiritual in every moment. But I can't help but wonder if the church would transform if we began to be more religious than spiritual. Claiming this posture, I believe, would lessen anxiety because once we did, there would be little to defend or prove.

Christ-Haunted

I've observed two kinds of structures in religion. First, a structure I can immerse myself in, such as a worship service or formation practice. Second, a structured theology that attempts to neatly answer questions. I'd guess that creatives like Cave often find structures of the second kind, that try to tie up answers with a bow, to be pedantic and rigid, kind of vapid.

Perhaps that's why, in an interview on Rick Rubin's *Tetragrammaton* podcast, Cave says he doesn't consider himself a Christian.[6] Still, I wonder how he would answer the question "Are you Christ-haunted?" à la Flannery O'Connor. Because I'm hard-pressed to think of anyone who sounds more Christ-haunted right now than Cave.

Cave experiences God by sitting down in a church. Rooney's character in *Beautiful World* does too. So have I. There is something that anyone, especially an aesthetically sensitive person, can experience while attending an artful service. Or when visiting a space that is awe-inspiring and sensing it is sanctified. God can meet us not by answering questions but by drawing us into beauty.

And yet, it seems so often that the opportunity is spoiled. It's heartbreaking that those of us who come up in church are in many cases becoming revolted by it. We are so far from where we want to be. The tenderhearted, creative people leaving church are in many cases fleeing because they have been failed. Again and again.

If followers of Jesus took Christianity more seriously as a religion and a spiritual practice and not just a cultural and political identifier, it could model to those in other faith traditions or in no faith tradition that there is something beautiful and generative in the Christian story that can be a balm to our anxious culture. We can hope that those hurt by church would find examples of Christians who have been transformed by faith and who lead differently because of the conviction of their belief.

Nonanxious Presence

Edwin Friedman, the late rabbi, therapist, and family systems theory expert, talks about modeling leadership within dysfunctional systems in his book *Failure of Nerve*. One of the ideas that he explores is that of nonanxious presence—that is, being calm during a time of panic. Nonanxious presence is not the central thesis of the book, but it is one of many important traits of a healthy leader.

About a decade ago, I became aware of nonanxious presence when our pastor John started talking to congregants about Friedman's systems work while exploring dynamics within his family of origin. Five years ago, another pastor friend started researching nonanxious presence for his doctoral thesis. Over the years, I found myself wondering how the concept, which seemed appealing but broad, could impact an individual personally.

Friedman first talked about the idea of being nonanxious in his 1985 book, *Generation to Generation: Family Process in Church and Synagogue*. He further developed his thinking around nonanxious presence in *Failure of Nerve*, published in 2007 after his death but largely written in the run-up to Y2K. At that time, the world was clearly anxious, but in many ways, Christians were in the dark about the causes of that anxiety. In 1999, the malignant spread of abuse and misuse of power committed by priests and pastors remained covered up or yet to be committed. From our current vantage point a quarter of the way into the twenty-first century, it's no wonder that

Friedman's thinking around nonanxious presence is experiencing a new resonance.

"My thesis here," Friedman writes, "is that the climate of contemporary America has become so chronically anxious that our society has gone into an emotional regression that is toxic to well-defined leadership."[7] When I read that, I thought, *Sir, you ain't seen nothing yet.*

I remember my nights on the porch watching Black Lives Matter protests, the moment I watched footage of the January 6 insurrection, and the Saturday of the assassination attempt against former President Trump resulting in a grazed ear. The frenzied, collective anxiety I tapped into during those moments was a sibling to internal worry about my body and the health of my parents. They are separate but complementary colors on an anxious wheel. I wondered, Did it have to feel this way? If there were nonanxious leaders in secular and sacred spaces, why were they hard to find? Could the church help?

Friedman focuses on how chronic anxiety metastasizes within systems. Nonanxious leaders have learned to model calm and offer it to others in times of panic, when it takes awareness and intention not to pass anxiety down. Mark Sayers writes, "By classifying anxiety as a personal issue rather than a systemic issue, we place an enormous burden on the individual, who then must modify their personal life to alleviate the suffering that anxiety brings."[8] We absorb our anxiety and everyone else's in a nervous system. I began to see that just as our anxiety can make others around us dysregulated and uneasy, so, too, nonanxious people can bear peace and calm in a way that others can sense and begin to metabolize.

I wonder, Would Sally Rooney's Alice and Nick Cave be drawn to the church if they sensed its anxiety? In a way, looking at church from the outside is a supreme benefit, having fresh eyes when so many of us are mired in its grievances.

Thinking about nonanxious presence led me to another question: How far has the virus of systemic anxiety spread? If creative newcomers could bring life back to the church and coax us into a quieting with beauty, they would be well-served by witnessing more examples of people who bear peace that manifests in religious as well as spiritual postures.

Then, like so many times before, I remembered that the work of becoming nonanxious is first an invitation to personal and possibly therapeutic work before we can model anything to another person. It requires interior and not broad thinking, remembering that it's up to God to sustain and protect the church. Any time we can find someone bearing a nonanxious presence, it is because of God's goodness shining through them onto us. Once again, it's about showing up and praying, *Christ, make me more like you.*

PART THREE

THE BODY POLITIC

13

Political Anxiety

I can think of a few reasons why evangelicals began to collapse into the arms of Donald Trump when he first ran for president in 2016, and one root cause: anxiety.

We want to be secure. Not homeless, not jobless, and not without health care. We would like to prevent real or imagined harm from coming to the people we love.

When we hear in speeches and interviews that we'll be kept safe from threats in a world with slim margins, we probably want to welcome it. In that sense, it was natural for evangelicals to believe Donald Trump's message that under his wing, Christian values will be restored. These promises to restore America as a Christian nation were thinly veiled attempts to win an election, and they offered wisps of safety and calmed many evangelical voters down. That kind of lip service, in modern America, was enough to, yet again, lure evangelical voters living on the defensive about a range of issues such as abortion, critical race theory, and book banning. Not to mention a tough job market, inflation, and threats to the social safety net.

Avoiding Anxiety Through Perceived Safety

The theological concept of the already and not yet—the idea that Jesus has declared the kingdom of God near while we wait for all to be made well when he returns—brings tension to the Christian life. The notion was introduced in the early 1900s by a theologian at Princeton named Geerhardus Vos.[1] It is one of the great mysteries of the church that God is living in us, is on earth with us, and is in a totally other realm.

It's difficult to live into the reality of the already and not yet in a complex political and cultural landscape, and some Christians can overcorrect, either by becoming immersed in culture or withdrawing from the world. Both reactions are attempts to avoid anxiety through perceived safety.

In 2024, data analyst Ryan Burge told *Christianity Today* editor-in-chief Russell Moore that mainline traditions began to shrink because they became indistinguishable from the rest of the world.[2] On the other end of the denominational spectrum, Burge found that the Southern Baptist Convention is also shrinking for another reason: Young people are tired of finding more messages of hate than welcome from the pulpit. The mainline perspective is to be in the world and of it, and the Baptist perspective is to be not in the world and not of it. Both are anxious.

Being set apart as a church—living in a way that is distinct from culture but active instead of withdrawn—could allow Christians to move toward unity in political and social differences with respect and cofacilitation. That, in theory, is true. Such unity, in practice, is far from reality.

A Climate of Anxiety

Political anxiety is not an official diagnosis in the Diagnostic and Statistical Manual of Mental Disorders (DSM), but it's an anecdotal condition that resonates with me and several peers. "Political anxiety is a term used to describe the recent increase in anxiety many people, regardless of party or political affiliation, are experiencing in the wake of the 2016 presidential election and in the current political climate in the United States. Also referred to as postelection stress, political anxiety is . . . a term that can be used in times of a stressful or divided political climate to reflect the reactions resulting from this turmoil."[3]

In the run up to the 2024 election, everyone I talked to seemed to be anxious about politics, whether we tended to use words such as "woke" and "coastal elite" for one party or "insurrectionist" and "alt-right" for the other party. A survey from the American Psychological Association found that "more than two-thirds of US adults (68%) say that the 2020 US presidential election is a significant source of stress in their life" across political affiliation. The percentage jumped 16 percent from the 2016 election.[4]

In evangelicalism, experiencing anxiety is like driving through a cloud of truck exhaust on the highway. You can close your window, but now smoke is also trapped inside. On one side of the glass is a great demoralization that has led to mass deconstruction and de-churching by a lot of hurt and weary people. On the other side of the glass is a politicized church in which voters are more entrenched and militant and are doubling down on nationalism.

I'm convinced the air can begin to clear in two ways. First, by embracing pluralism to protect the freedom of religious liberty for people of all and no faith traditions. Second, by pursuing an earthy holiness, living in a way that manifests the fruits of the spirit and is inspired by the teachings of Jesus.

COeXisT

In high school, I dated a student who lived on campus at a Lutheran seminary while his father finished his doctorate. Raised a red-blooded evangelical of the nondenominational variety and not in a eucharistic tradition like my boyfriend's, I found the call-and-response worship and organ hymns boring and forgettable when attending Lutheran services with his family. It would be years until I'd find mystery and comfort in liturgical traditions. But I learned one value from my boyfriend's seminarian dad that stayed with me over the decades: Christians should work to protect the separation of church and state and foster a society where, regardless of what we believe, everyone has equal dignity.

After Joe Biden exited the 2024 presidential race and Kamala Harris quickly built momentum around her campaign as the Democratic nominee, Trump courted the evangelical vote with increasing desperation, delivering this comment at a Florida fundraiser: "Christians, get out and vote, just this time. You won't have to do it anymore. Four more years, you know what, it will be fixed, it will be fine, and you won't have to vote anymore, my beautiful Christians."[5]

At the Faith & Freedom Coalition the month prior, Trump implored a group of evangelicals to "go and vote, Christians, please!" The remarks came days after Louisiana became the sole state in the US to legally require every public school classroom to display the Ten Commandments. "Has anyone read the 'Thou shalt not steal'? I mean, has anybody read this incredible stuff? It's just incredible," Trump told the coalition. "They don't want it to go up. It's a crazy world."[6]

This posturing sounds like a pickup line: "Do you come here often? Can I buy you another rum and Coke? Do you know I love the Ten Commandments?" Trump followed up by posting in all caps on social media: "I LOVE THE TEN COMMANDMENTS IN PUBLIC SCHOOLS, PRIVATE SCHOOLS, AND MANY OTHER PLACES, FOR THAT MATTER. READ IT—HOW CAN WE, AS A NATION, GO WRONG???"[7]

I imagine the Ten Commandments in "many other places," scrawled out on bathroom stall walls, gym lockers, and skate parks.

According to the Aspen Institute, religious pluralism "is the state of being where every individual in a religiously diverse society has the rights, freedoms, and safety to worship, or not, according to their conscience."[8] Remember, in the family I grew up in, we believed that Christianity was a way of life and not a religion. We were suspicious of efforts toward pluralism because it seemed like a slippery slope to slapping a "coexist" bumper sticker on our car, the word COEXIST spelled with various religious imagery: a peace sign in the place of the letter *O*, a Star of David in the place of the letter *X*, and a cross in the place of the letter *T*. Like a lot of evangelical families in the '90s, we were much more focused on abstinence pledges than pluralism. My parents would have celebrated Louisiana's decision to display the Ten Commandments at my neighborhood public school.

As I moved into adulthood, I began to more deeply understand how, as a Christian, pluralism is not just allowable but also essential to the health of a nation like the United States. Supporting pluralism resists Christian nationalism and its threat to American democracy by declaring America as God's chosen nation with a special blessing. Pluralism offers hope for an American church whose witness has been tarnished by white nationalist rhetoric co-opting Christian language to condone hate.

My high school boyfriend's dad was a conservative Lutheran pastor, but he was on a soapbox for the separation of church and state because he understood something a lot of his peers probably overlooked: Pluralism preserves the right to practice Christianity across denominations, and it requires the same right of full and free religious practice to all citizens. If people of other religions don't have the right to worship freely, neither do we.

Pluralism emerged during the Protestant Reformation in Europe in the sixteenth century. It was a response to the religious status quo and conflict caused by institutions that too closely aligned with the state. Various groups of Christians seeking to practice in distinct ways had emerged across Europe, and America became a refuge for waves of people fleeing religious violence and seeking a place to worship, including Quakers, Catholics, Puritans, and Anabaptists.

Unfortunately, a rising number of Americans don't think about how democracy is weakened as pluralism declines. A

2022 Pew study reported that "about a third of US adults who say the US should be a Christian nation (32%) also think the fact that the country is religiously diverse—i.e., made up of people from many different religions as well as people who are not religious—weakens American society."[9] I can't help but think that the undercurrent of the belief that Christianity loses power when other religions are tolerated is linked to racism and fear of the other.

Christian nationalism calls for America to be Christianized. In contrast, pluralism neutralizes any claim that there is a single right culture or nation. This dovetails with the message of the gospel, which teaches that God created and is for all nations.

The reciprocal ethic of Jesus calls Christians to "love your neighbor as yourself" (Matt. 22:39). That doesn't just mean Christian neighbors. If we desire freedom to worship as we feel led, it follows that we should extend to our neighbor the freedom to practice faith according to their conscience, or not at all.

Slapping the Ten Commandments on classroom walls to show dominance is an anxiety response rooted in the fear of no longer directing the discourse. If you don't believe in pluralism, there is no choice other than to grasp for dominance to maintain the freedom to worship. But the opposite is true. If we lean into the pluralism America was founded on, we don't have to fight for control.

The truth is, none of us fully understand the powers and factors at play in this world, let alone the world to come. James writes, "Humble yourselves before the Lord, and he will lift you up" (James 4:10). When we acknowledge that we all act in faith, either to believe or not to believe, we welcome humility. People following Jesus's teachings are called by God to believe that love, not political anxiety, is active, healing, and our best hope for unity.

Upholding the spirit of pluralism lets Christians lay down any anxious need to dominate out of the fear that we might one day lose control that was never ours to begin with. In doing so, we give up power to whom it belongs: God.

Less Literate

I read political news like some people read the sports section: closely tracking polls, passionately scanning campaign updates on fundraising goals and celebrity endorsements. I'm into politics; I'm mildly wonky. However, after my anxiety spiked during the 2024 election season, it became clear that I needed to deprioritize political consumption and instead prioritize loving and serving the people in my local sphere. I needed to rightsize my relationship with politics and accept what I can and cannot control.

I soon found that letting go of the grip of politics felt a bit like losing an identity marker. To be politically literate and up on breaking news signals the perception of being relevant, of being a global citizen, which some of us crave. That's not inherently bad, of course. But I had to remind myself that as a Christian, I'm called first to find my identity in Christ (see Gal. 3:26–28).

Amid the unending breaking news of America's politics, I find solace in Christianity. It models how we can have hope in a bigger story and allows us to reprioritize the role of politics in our lives. If "the worst" happens politically, whatever that looks like, there are still other important things to cling to. This is certainly true for those who are white, housed, educated, and not at risk of deportation or the loss of vital social services. There is little to lose for people like me and so much on the line for millions of others. No matter who we are and regardless of the outcome of any election, we can continue to care for our community and engage in local issues, supporting people who are unhoused, refugees, migrants, and others who may become even more vulnerable depending on who sits in the Oval Office or on the Supreme Court.

It is possible for Christians to be nonanxious about the implications of any oppressive administration. Living well, regardless of political leadership, is a form of resistance that honors where God has placed us. By living well, I do not mean being comfortable. I mean being present and of service. Rather than staying stuck in stress about the future of our country, we are free, wherever we are, to let ourselves be set apart to offer solidarity and care.

Becoming Holy

I googled something like "What is the true meaning of holiness" and got the following answer: "The quality or state of being holy."[10] It made me laugh. The unhelpful definition also confirmed a suspicion: For many people, holiness is inaccessible and difficult to grasp, a privileged pursuit typically involving a hermitage and a patron. I associate holiness with a posture reserved for hermits—or the retirees hiking the Camino de Santiago. Holiness is a dreamlike reality we can't afford. Plus, isn't it indulgent to begin a pursuit of holiness in a world that feels like it is falling apart?

And yet history tells us this isn't the case. In the precarious time of the Vikings when slaughtering and raiding were common, early Irish missionaries entered areas of violence when it was not required to bring peace and bear witness to God's love. Many of us today can't fathom making the same decision. That strength, using words instead of weapons, requires a serious pursuit of holiness.

Holiness simply means being set apart.

The American church is not set apart well. Instead of being a light drawing people to live gently, lovingly, and with self-control, the church is institutionally anxious. At the time I am writing this, countless congregants have been harmed by abuse and the celebrification of the pulpit. Pastors are still burned out from the pandemic, funding for faith-based humanitarian organizations is being slashed, and nationalism is revealing the stark divide between fake political Christianity and the way of Jesus. Systemic anxiety in the church has harmed our collective potential for holiness.

Holiness is more communal than most of us think. In pure form, the biblical call to holiness is a collective call for a set-apart community. Holiness should be attractive at a gut level because it is about restoring our noble creational intent before the fall, being fully human in the world, and being broken healers with our words and work.

Thinking about this, I began to envision holiness not as something experienced at the mountaintop but at the kitchen table, on the commute, and in the middle-of-the-night haze.

At many points in history—and in parts of the world today—people have faced life-threatening afflictions that offer the mess of modern American politics needed perspective. This is our time and place, and we can only endure if we truly believe in an eschatology that says things may well go to hell but the church will remain. We have been set apart for a reason. Personal and political outcomes will never be predictable during our lifetime. But no matter what may come, there is steady hope for the future flourishing of the kingdom. In God's good future, all will be accounted for. Christians can find a little more strength if we face losing everything because we believe that in the end, nothing that is of value will be lost. We will not have lived and loved in vain.

Grazed and Confused

In the past month of writing this book, former president Trump was grazed by a bullet in an assassination attempt, and he emerged at the Republican National Convention wearing an ear bandage. Several delegates in the crowd mirrored this in a show of solidarity. A stadium studded with ear patches. Meanwhile, President Biden stepped down as the presumptive Democratic nominee and Vice President Kamala Harris stepped up and quickly united her party, naming Minnesota Governor Tim Walz as her pick for vice president. A growing momentum of joy emerged, complete with memes and excitement from Gen Z. That month alone brought constant instability and political whiplash.

Before the 2024 election, AND Campaign founder Justin Giboney gave a talk at a university about being "more faithful in the public square."[11] Political anxiety is stoked when we are not well-formed and spiritually mature. Giboney referenced Ephesians 4:

> Then we will no longer be infants, tossed back and forth by the waves, and blown here and there by every wind of teaching and by the cunning and craftiness of people in their deceitful

> scheming. Instead, speaking the truth in love, we will grow to become in every respect the mature body of him who is the head, that is, Christ. From him the whole body, joined and held together by every supporting ligament, grows and builds itself up in love, as each part does its work. (vv. 14–16)

Modeling calm in political turmoil invites Christians to move from milk to solid food (see 1 Cor. 3:2), from living in infant bodies to adult bodies. Doing so requires us to move past snap judgments in order to see the dignity in all people. "The only way to see God in someone who hates you is to see what's invisible outside of faith. . . . You have to want to see it. Sometimes you have to be willing to imagine it in spite of their behavior and all other indications. That's Christian," Giboney says. "It's the difference between wanting vengeance and wanting redemption."[12] It's the difference between taking an anxious stance of defense or an openhanded stance of holding space for people across the political spectrum.

James Davison Hunter, the sociologist credited with coining the phrase "culture war," has seen the dehumanization of those across the aisle for decades. "We live in a space where our politics and our moralities are so abstract and symbolic that we lose sight of the human beings that are hidden in plain sight behind them," he said. Instead, Hunter says Christians can be faithful presences as "a way of conceiving not only theology but an incarnational ethic that allows us to address the problems that are right in front of us, embodied in human beings who are just hurting." Hunter calls for embodied hope on behalf of the other, for more people to emerge who are "willing to suffer on behalf"[13] of the other to infuse hope for all.

Hands and Feet

Drew and Asher spent the January morning of the 2025 inauguration at a community P-Patch for refugees operated by a resettlement agency. Some of the people who grow greens and spices in these plots were threatened with deportation. I imagine the cilantro growing wild to coriander seed, untended.

I think a lot about the gap between bleak and scary news coming out of the Capitol and daily life: weeding a P-Patch, dishing bowls of rice for a volunteer lunch after the workday. As anxiety swirls, we can do good work, and that's something.

We are living in an era of immense instability and uncertainty. The cuts to global aid, defunding of vital federal services and supports, and mass layoffs announced in the weeks after the inauguration are harrowing. Each day feels unprecedented. We haven't seen anything like it in our lifetime. The news keeps coming.

"What future is there for our politics? For our churches? For us?" Michael Wear asks. "Our politics has no answers it does not first receive from us. At the center of our faith is not a series of right answers, but a person. This is what we have to offer our politics: the kind of person we are."[14] Change in our politics has to start by asking God to heal the hurt and fear in our hearts and continue by using our hands. This kind of solidarity work is rooted, steady. Whatever may come, serving as the hands and feet of Jesus is not conceptual; it is formative and essential.

14

Already, Not Yet

Being in and not of the world is hard when you never fully lived in it to begin with. That's why Christians raised to expect a single, central conversion moment like I was might long for something to be converted *from*—to have had a past to be saved out of—for the change to faith to be more real.

As a Christian kid, being in and not of the world meant going to the sleepover but sitting out the games I was told might conjure the demonic, such as "light as a feather, stiff as a board." As a teen and co-ed, it meant smoking a single clove but not buying a pack, indulgent but light; swearing but only when a swear word came up in song lyrics; taking a sip of beer foam but not drinking a pint.

It meant making out in the little car on a dead-end Indiana road but stopping after an hour. I'd sleep next to boys but not with them. I'd listen to Riot Grrrls but never move to Olympia and join a band. I signed an agreement when I enrolled at an evangelical university at age eighteen saying I wouldn't drink, but I had a few screwdrivers at a bar in the closest city to campus after I turned twenty-one. My friends did mostly the same.

Bored during the pandemic, my friend Zack found old footage on YouTube of concerts he'd attended with friends in the early 2000s, including a Fugazi show in Louisville. There they were in the crowd, my friends in their midtwenties bodies. I paused the video when there was a view of my best friend, looking doe-eyed and awkward around kids moshing and crowd surfing. If I had been next to her in the video, I would have had the same look on my face.

I skimmed the surface of culture when I was an adolescent and beyond, but I did not immerse myself in it. For a long time into adulthood, I did not understand how—and as a response to God's abundant love—I could be a fully free person and experience pleasure. I mean abundant, sweet-ripe-fruit indulgences while mindfully practicing healthy self-discipline and denial. I was guilted into being good, and my reaction was often half-assed attempts toward an unbridled worldliness that, at least in my thought life, trickled into adulthood. This was less than ideal.

On the other hand, I saw how my tempered worldliness gave me a broader vantage point to question whether evangelicalism was a place where everyone was safe from the world's dangers. As an emerging adult, I could not have told you that patriarchy, abuse of power, performative holiness, and a pastoral cult of personality made evangelical culture seem like something to keep a distance from. The industry of American Christendom had not been obvious to me either. But my friends and I had sensed that something was askew. I didn't belong in evangelical culture, and I was hesitant to fully belong in the world. Jesus remained compelling but not central.

In some sense, scrupulous tendencies and rigid morals kept me away from imagined carnality to the point where any theoretical deviance I heard about in the '90s became preemptively not for me—threesomes and ecstasy at a rave, much less today's iterations such as open relationships and psilocybins. And so I experienced the world more in my mind than in my body. While in my youth, I did not have a theology for my lack of immersion in the wide world—and fear kept me from it. I did have an intuition that hot, fleshy things could end poorly and become sad. I wondered whether other people experienced these things only theoretically, in their head, because they might regret a choice later. Maybe I was wise and God protected me. Maybe I was judgmental and scared.

Not of It

By the time I had a family, my well-worn pattern of not living apart as a Christian while also not fully living in the world was failing because I was tired. I thought about removing myself from the world completely. I read Rod Dreher's *The Benedict Option* and wondered if I should "embrace exile from the mainstream culture and construct a resilient counterculture."[1] I thought that maybe forming a safe enclave would bring relief, until I realized that this kind of relief could only be found if you could afford it and were not interested in contributing to the flourishing of anyone outside your bubble.

A few years later, I read about tradwives, or traditional wives. The subculture of these conservative Christian and

Mormon women was covered extensively by the media. Tradwifery content is highly consumable by the general public because it is so unlike many of our experiences.

Tradwives usually enjoy enough financial stability from their spouses to not work and willingly adopt conventional gender roles. The idealization of "old-fashioned" ways of life, such as homesteading, is riveting to tradwives. I remember reading the Eric Carle board book *Pancakes! Pancakes!* with Asher when he was a toddler. In the story, Jack wants a pancake for breakfast. "But first, Jack's mother needs flour from the mill, an egg from the black hen, milk from the spotted cow, butter churned from fresh cream, and firewood for the stove."[2]

In my early parenting years, I could barely muster the energy to flip a passable Saturday morning stack of pancakes from a Trader Joe's box mix. The story of Jack and his mother was set on a farm fairyland where you worked hard for your pancakes, and they are hearty and delicious because of the extra effort. Tradwives are up for the challenge of milking, churning, grinding, flipping, and serving hungry mouths—and looking picture-perfect while doing it. Regular moms wipe off counters dusted in flour from the box.

I found several common themes as I scrolled through social media posts with #tradwife, and most included the kitchen. One woman is pictured in a linen apron with a wooden spoon at a butcher block counter, her children surrounding her. Another woman is shown with her back to the camera in a long prairie dress, hair down, floofing a vase of baby's breath. The caption explains that it's a blessing men and women are not the same, and then it goes on to clarify that while the man's role is to protect the family, the woman's is to multiply it.

I wondered if I could ever become a tradwife. "These women extol a 50s escapist fantasy of 'chastity, marriage, motherhood,' a fantasy that Betty Friedan famously exposed as 'magical thinking' in *The Feminine Mystique*."[3] Before I had kids, I would daydream about being home with a toddler like my mom was with me. Six months after Asher was born, though, I was glad to have a quiet, organized desk to go to during the day at a small publisher and coworkers who wanted to talk about production schedules and print runs instead of tummy time and sleep training.

Later, when Asher was in preschool, there was a stint when I wanted to run an organic baby food business. I googled "community kitchen space Seattle" and imagined the freedom of days spent listening to loud music while chopping, boiling, and straining locally harvested plums. It took little more to shake me out of the daydream than making an appointment with a foodborne illness attorney to discuss the liability of product recalls that could make a baby sick.

Then when my son was a year old, I left my job at the publisher and tried to write remote "online content" and manage social media for a couple of record labels. I had another baby and wanted domestic labor and desk work to live together under an 850-square-foot roof. I thought that arrangement was best for the kids. I'd idealized a version of at-home motherhood because my mom had stayed home, even though it didn't fit my pace.

At one point, I tried working for a few months at a community cooking school, lured by the promise of helping the owner write a cookbook. On my first day, I polished silverware, bumped my head in the attic looking for obscurely shaped bundt pans, and lugged alt flours from an outdoor storage space to the teaching kitchen. After shattering glassware and spilling coffee, it was clear that my dream of life away from the desk and working with my hands did not dovetail with my clumsy disposition. That was my last attempt at combining a work-from-home and domestic career. By that point, I felt too old and tired to fantasize about a life I theoretically wanted to be good at.

Relevance and Power

It's tempting to poke fun at #tradwife culture over a pint at happy hour. But kneading dough and milking cows is not something we could all do, or do well, regardless of resources or values. If you are a tradwife, you probably feel like you're working toward a healthy, wholesome calling. To be honest, I'm a little bit in awe of a woman who can carve out the kind of life that requires working with your hands with skills I don't have access to, even if I'm not interested in cultivating them.

But there is also a political side to tradwifery. I'd wager that many tradwives don't think about the politicization of the culture, but some subsets know exactly what they are messaging. An early adopter of the movement was British tradwife Alena Kate Pettitt, whose "family often found themselves unable to eat the homemade banana bread until she had captured it adequately for her feed." Pettitt became disillusioned and has since left the subculture and her sizable social media following, telling *The New Yorker* how she "watched the rise of the younger trad wives with fascination, then alarm. 'It's become an aesthetic, and then it's become politicized,' she said, of the movement in its new era. 'And then it's become its own monster.'"[4]

By 2022, "the movement appeared to be turning into something between a money-making exercise and an amped-up, kink version of cottagecore with political and religious overtones." But it still has plenty of adherents, drawn to tradwifery's "deftly curated social-media fantasy, lured, perhaps, by the hustle of the anti-hustle, the opt-out from job dissatisfaction and economic insecurity, or tempted by the promise of a single, coherent identity gathered around a distant, simpler time."[5] I wondered if there is any way to be "not of the world" and also leverage it online. Does the public display of maternal bliss disqualify tradwives from living differently? Well, yes. Because if we can always watch, they will always perform and eventually coalesce around cultural and political identity markers. It's the American way.

Tradwife culture supports natalism, having more children, in "a revived push to organize American public policy around childbearing."[6] Pro-natalists support the idea that Americans should have more children to reverse a declining birth rate, an argument that has gained momentum on both sides of the political aisle for different reasons. The left may see a drive to increase the birth rate as a possible way to make headway on family-centric policy that supports working parents, such as universal pre-K and paid maternity leave. In contrast, some members of the right are eager to push natalist views for nefarious reasons that make conservative white tradwives natural advocates[7]—namely, to Make America White Again.

Many tradwives see feminism as backfiring against the white nuclear family by taking women out of the home. "This narrative also laments how white men have been robbed of their rightful status; their jobs and roles have been taken by women, people of color, and immigrants in the workforce."[8]

Some tradwives are a part of "what's been called the 'crunchy to alt-right pipeline,' where granola-fueled enthusiasm for organic farming, fermentation or homeschooling (none of which—obviously!—is inherently alt-right) elides into anti-vaxxing, decrying contraception and woke liberal modernity."[9] These women are politically postured to rally around family values with their social media accounts and their votes.

There is a cadre of Mormon tradwife influencers. Some conservative Catholics also embody tradwife ideals. These Catholic women may move beyond homesteading and homeschooling ideals to modeling life around Mary, the mother of God. "It is this performance of hyper-femininity that allows Catholic tradwives to conflate themselves with a self-sacrificial Mary. Her emphatic yes at the Annunciation is the model of submission to God and to men, her motherhood is seen as her divine vocation, and, thus, Mary becomes the ideal Catholic trad wife," Emma Cieslik writes in the *National Catholic Reporter*.[10]

The same through line is traced from tradwife culture to the evangelical purity culture of the '80s and '90s, which promoted abstinence before marriage. We're all looking for our people, the market is looking for money, and more conservative strains of religion—be it evangelical, Catholic, or Mormon flavor—is looking for relevance and political power. These sorts of movements rarely end well. The next generation of kids who grow up in ultraconservative households are often the most hurt.

While both tradwife and purity cultures value chastity, purity culture reached wider and trickled up to Hollywood, with celebrity spokespeople declaring that they would stay virgins until marriage. Purity culture was accessible to all genders, and signing an abstinence pledge was arguably more ecumenical than aspirational homesteading. Eventually, tradwives will fade from the cultural conversation just as purity culture did.

New Piety

Shortly after the 2024 election, James Pogue talked about masculinity, self-help, and the New Right on *The Ezra Klein Show*. In the podcast conversation, Pogue discusses the pull toward yeomanry. Yeomanry originally referred to middle-class farmers who owned small amounts of land in nineteenth-century England and served as a second line of defense in the military. Some conservative men today are essentially appropriating this centuries-old status, drawn to the self-sufficient masculinity it evokes.

Klein notes how in the run-up to the last election, interest in spartan-esque masculinity of the past swelled—to a time when "men could be men."[11] This version of America hearkens back to an earlier time when all men were, as the story goes, eager to enlist in the military and die for country to protect their land.

Put together, tradwives and yeoman paint a picture of new piety. A landscape for over the mantel of farmsteading mothers working alongside cattle-raising husbands. Come hell or high water, they are prepared on their own acreage. In this American fantasy, every man is paired with a self-sufficient and all-natural woman. And no one is going to force-feed pasteurized milk down their throats or shoot RSV vaccines in their kids' arms.

Set Apart

When I was growing up in northeast Indiana, we had to drive only five minutes north to find horses pulling buggies and fields of Amish kids wearing bonnets. In Brooklyn, I've wandered through Hasidic communities where walk-up balconies become sukkot tents and streets are lined with school buses with Hebrew on the side. The small taste I've had of these worlds was enough to cue a clear message: They were not intended for me or anyone I knew but for a specific group of designated people. A high fence was built around these opaque communities, and any sexual or spiritual abuse, mental illness, or addiction that occurred was dealt with, or gaslit, privately.

In a healthy scenario, part of these groups' longevity includes the high value placed on community. What can Christians learn from them about being a distinctive people, living set apart yet engaged in the world?

The members of these communities live in the US, but they are also differentiated from it. When Jesus was on earth, he lived in the Middle East but was a citizen of heaven. I like the idea of being a citizen of the world while we are here but with a sojourner's posture. I wondered how to carry a sense of home as a citizen of heaven.

Theologian Dallas Willard considers the already-and-not-yet reality of God's kingdom in how we live on earth, holding the tension between this age and the age to come. Willard argues that living as citizens of heaven can be easily corrupted if we "'invest solely' in matters of the flesh," and he says flesh and desire work together naturally and can become obsessive. An anxious desire that searches and wants for gain is lust.

"The terrible 'deeds of the flesh'—sexual immorality, impurity, sensuality, idolatry, sorcery, enmities, strife, jealousy, outbursts of anger, disputes, dissensions, factions, envying, drunkenness, carousing, and things like these . . . are the natural and inevitable outcomes of 'lusts.'"[12]

To resist destructive will rooted in desire, Willard calls for surrender through spiritual disciplines that allow Christians to walk with the Holy Spirit, "such as solitude, silence, fasting, study, worship, service, and so forth, to quell our desires that have been running our life and embed the will of Christ into our body."[13] This is the kind of fruit in the Christian life that brings spiritual rest, moves us toward healthy community, and empties us of false desire.

Author Jen Pollock Michel writes deftly about taking a wrong approach to resisting desire. "I was deeply afraid that given an inch when it came to desire, I would take the unholy mile. I thought of sanctification, not as a *hallowing* of the self (and its inevitable life of desiring) but as a *hollowing*. All the bowels of my humanness would be spooned out, and I would be filled with one robotic desire and one desire alone: for the will of God."[14]

Pollock Michel warns against an overcorrection of the will that leads to forbiddance, which "posits all desire as selfish and sinful. This is generally the error of overly zealous religious people. They have so little faith in the good, deep, slow work that God is doing in his people, and they have so little imagination for the maturity of wisdom as it forms. They would rather avoid a risk rather than make a mistake."[15]

I can relate. As a young adult, I didn't indulge because of forbiddance. I carried a sense, like Pollock Michel, that "being good" was the same as pursuing a healthy holiness.

Even though I withheld from worldliness while indulging in as much as I felt safe to explore, I was "good" for the wrong reasons. Practicing spiritual disciplines offers us a different path. As we grow, we can develop better faculties and understand that God desires Christians to pursue an earthy holiness precisely because of the freedom it offers.

Behind my house, below the porch, there is a small stone path next to an oversize rhododendron and camellia that leads to the yard. In the late spring, I stand next to the house on the path, pick dropped flowers, and close my eyes. Sometimes, I'm next to the path under the trees. Sometimes, my back is against the house. A gentle call to realignment. The metaphor, when it came, was so obvious I almost couldn't receive it. "For the gate is narrow" (Matt. 7:14 NRSV).

All the longing, the freedom I craved and enjoyed as a young adult, is in me. I am not a perfect woman. I am not wild and free. I rarely work with my hands. I am hovering around a narrow path, and I'll spend the rest of my life finding it, losing the trail, and finding my way back. A longing for the desire to be set apart came on good days. As the seasons changed, as my face and body moved closer to my mom than my young self, my job was to be faithful and present.

15

Evangelical Anxiety

After living in Seattle for more than a decade, Drew and I talked about whether to return to Indiana. Friends from church sat with us for several meetings in a Quaker clearness committee–style, asking open-ended questions such as, “What would you most like about living in the Midwest again? What would you leave behind if you left?”

During that discernment process, we returned to Indiana a couple of times to revisit the community we'd left in 2004. We met with friends and listened to their stories about how the area had struggled and grown. After nine months, we found repeated consolation in the decision to remain in Seattle. The day we decided not to move, I experienced a deep sense of confirmation that let me settle down. In staying, I became less anxious.

A similar release happened one other time in my life when I was in my twenties. Drew and I dated for six years before we married. After a lot of uncertainty, we decided we'd spend our lives together. My shoulders loosened after the wedding. My posture changed.

I can see a similar path unfolding in a slower, steadier beat over the last decade in my Christian practice. After trying to manage a Christian identity I didn't talk about for years because I was worried about how friends would receive me, I decided to move toward Jesus. That was in 2017, around the same time we decided to stay in Seattle. I let go of the need to control how people might view me—be it too "woke" or too conservative or whatever. I just let it be. I let my belief morph and grow but did not question it as central. Perhaps not coincidentally, this season of my life overlapped in politics with both Donald Trump's presidency and deconstruction culture in the church.

Left Behind, Again

That old left-behind feeling? It's one I knew well. The fear of being left behind in my rapture-ready childhood was similar to my real-life experience starting in my twenties of being left behind by friends who departed from the faith. I understood the precise interior alienation when you believe things your friends stopped believing or loosened their grip on.

I felt these same familiar waves of isolation in the church's current deconstruction era, which picked up speed after the 2016 US presidential election when many peers started to question and look closer at why they believed what they did about Christianity. Maybe having navigated feelings of isolation and spiritual estrangement from friends earlier on was an inoculation for this season of loss, Drew and I wondered.

Years later, I have to ask harder questions: Did I begin writing about my faith out of grief, or assuming the role of a grizzled Christian who had "stayed true" with a tinge of superiority? Was my sadness a tug of the Holy Spirit, or an anxious reaction to becoming even more culturally obscured because I stayed in the church?

The Black, queer, Christian writer Talique Taylor wrote about being failed by both evangelicalism and "exvangelicalism," loosely defined as people who have left the evangelical church. Taylor said, "[My] church experience had taught me spiritual superiority, my exvangelical experience taught me intellectual and moral superiority. It was always about condemning the other."[1] Were Drew and I managing both postures—the culturally relevant intellectuals and the church loyalists? Were there wisps of spiritual and moral smugness in how we felt about friends who left the church?

A dangerous thing can happen when we are one of the few people we know who still identify as Christian: judgment cloaked in compassion. Perhaps we say we saw the slippery slope of this or that person's faith coming. It's the bubble gum inside the Blow Pop, a sweet vindication in being correct in our prediction. It's also artificial, a power play to self-soothe.

Many of us still in the church have done a good job of making deconstruction into an us versus them thing. Instead of listening and loving, Christians fixated on the deconstruction conversation might be just as siloed from the other side of the aisle as folks at a Trump rally who are against the liberal elite. Or who were at a Harris rally, for that matter.

Maybe the word "deconstruction" has lost a sense of subversiveness. Maybe it did awhile ago.

However, the assumptions by one kind of Christian about another—the judgments—have not stopped. This is a human thing we do in our heads. We put people in buckets because we're nervous, and it shows.

Deconstructing Deconstruction

You can probably tell when somebody talks casually about deconstruction but is nervous and trying to sound cool with it, *no biggie*. You can also tell when ultraright evangelicals use the word as political ammunition to pump a base of nationalists or to sell books. Sometimes, people use the word because it fits as a way to talk about the choice to leave evangelicalism. Still other people use the word to express their dark night of the soul: an age-old trial that has always been a vital part of belief. I've distanced myself from the word "deconstruction" because it doesn't feel true to my experience, preferring terms like "spiritual desert" to discuss my seasons of doubt in order to be inclusive and "literary."

My own experience of "spiritual disorientation" (also "literary") happened a long time ago, and it felt quiet. I didn't have the language to back up what was happening to me. Thanks to the contemplative tradition, I do now: "a long desolation."

I came out of it a little bloodied and busted up. It lasted more than a decade and required a great deal of work to maintain multiple identities that I'd burned out on. At this point, I'm "hemmed into" Jesus. It may sound gory, but I would crawl under his holy skin and call it a blanket. I am a Jesus person. I should have lived in the '60s.

I can tell you there is nothing I can do at this point to unhem myself from Jesus. As much as I hide, deflect, get bored, get embarrassed, kick, or scream, Jesus is the calm friend on the couch. "Do you want to get a coffee?" he asks. "Or a whisky. Let's talk it out." I pray a bit, sit in silence, and feel better. The chaos around wanting to jettison my faith is centered on the self. The settling down is where I can get over myself and be more present in caring for other people.

That may be true about my individual life as a Christian. But what about the larger tradition in which I and many peers were raised?

The "Evangelical" Question

I've been thinking about the question of evangelicalism for some years—specifically, about the use of that word. My thinking is like that of many other Christians. We are trying to figure out what to call ourselves or not call ourselves and what we anxiously gain or lose by association.

Growing up, no one I knew thought about the term "evangelical." It was used synonymously with "protestant" in my circles. Instead, questions of identity were about character, about becoming a stronger Christian. Because if we *really believed*, if we had enough faith, we would not need counseling in a mental health crisis. God would heal. When that didn't work, believers in my community could seek help from "Christian counselors," even though I never understood the difference between them and therapists. Dad, who is in deep need of mental health support for anxiety and the stress of caregiving, will not seek it still today.

Charles Marsh, a professor of religious studies at the University of Virginia, was interviewed in *Rolling Stone* about his memoir *Evangelical Anxiety*. Marsh found a way forward in therapy, and the reporter asked him, "Why don't more 'recovering Christians,' as they've been called, seek out the sort of grace you did?"

Marsh responded:

> I mean, the white evangelical project is wracked by inner anxieties, but [for many] it feels that it would be somehow unholy or unseemly, if not even sinful, to interrogate those inner anxieties. There is still a pervasive fear of the psyche and a sense that most mental health problems, depression, and anxiety in particular, may find some relief through talk or medication, but their real source is a spiritual lack, an absence of a certain kind of commitment to the disciplines of the Christian life.[2]

Like Marsh, the evangelicalism of my youth messaged that if I was a better Christian, I would be fully cured of anxiety. Therapy was only required if my faith wasn't strong enough. As a result, my evangelical identity spiked my anxiety because I believed I was not faithful enough to qualify for full healing. Could the better Christian find complete relief?

The reason why I cannot relate to evangelicalism is not just about the movement's political corruption and egregious acts. It is about the undertones of a portion of evangelical culture telling us to try harder, that we are special and protected from affliction. But I've only moved closer to Jesus through embracing affliction, not believing I deserve an exemption. That's magical thinking.

Still, what brought me to the question of whether I am an evangelical was not only a personal matter but also a cultural one.

I read Ruth Graham's 2024 *New York Times* piece "Piety and Profanity: The Raunchy Christians Are Here" about the "Conservative Dad's Real Women of America" calendar sponsored by a "woke free" beer company. Graham writes:

> A raunchy, outsider, boobs-and-booze ethos has elbowed its way into the conservative power class, accelerated by the rise of Donald J. Trump, the declining influence of traditional religious institutions and a shifting media landscape increasingly dominated by the looser standards of online culture . . .
>
> But for some conservative Christians, the stakes of the moment are now high enough that a certain amount of vulgarity is not just tolerated, but also required as a form of truth-telling worthy of the prophets.[3]

I read the article and felt in my gut that evangelicalism may be beyond repair. The gut feel was similar to drinking a cherry slushie before riding a roller coaster, then getting sick. I thought, *There is only so much we can handle before evangelicalism is lost in a morass of strange morals and messages.*

Historian Kristin Kobes Du Mez was interviewed for the piece, noting that raunchy Christian culture is gaining acceptance. There is, Graham writes, "a moment of deep conservative outrage, an often visceral disgust, at rising rates of nontraditional gender and sexual identities, particularly among young people. In that context, an indulgence in heterosexual lust, even if in poor taste, is becoming seen as not just benign, but maybe even healthy and noble."[4]

Kobes Du Mez concurs, "Against that backdrop, it's a wholesome thing for a boy to be lusting after a very sexy woman."[5]

The message this calendar is telling, or rather selling, is anti-Christian. And I don't know if there is anything to be done to stop the wave of white-hot, angry, red-white-and-blue evangelicalism that is behind it.

That same day, after reading Graham's article, I also read Michael C. Bender's reporting on "The Church of Trump: How He's Infusing Christianity into His Movement." Trump rallies around the 2016 election used to feature frequent QAnon finger raises from the crowd, Bender reports, a signal to other voters in the stadium that you were in on the far-right conspiracy. In 2024, there was less QAnon ephemera in audiences and more hands raised in worship. A video embedded in the article shows how the end of a Trump rally is like a church service. People get quiet and listen to their prophet.[6]

Reading articles like these, I think, *God, can I still do this?* Is it a test of will or a point of pride to call myself an evangelical because I don't like jettisoning identifiers? Or because I've never really "felt" like an evangelical as a creative, arty teen onward?

Three Responses

After reading the Graham and Bender articles, I could think of only three responses a reasonable person could make to "the Trumpification of the church" illustrated in those two articles and many others like them that ran in the months leading up to the 2024 election:

1. Check out of politics and ignore its impact on the church.
2. Distance yourself.
3. Vocally and aggressively push back.

I found Drew in the kitchen and told him about these articles and the fresh waves of hopelessness I felt after reading them. Having a person like Drew to talk to—someone of relentless optimism and thoughtfulness—is a gift. Sometimes his stubborn hope pisses me off. I once thought that no one could be so clear-eyed unless they were out of touch. Then I realized that Drew is as "in touch" as I'd like to think I am. He's politically fluent, theologically trained, and culturally grounded. He calms me down.

I was wearing thin when I went to Drew, not just about evangelicalism but also the state of broader Christianity. I read him the articles and shared my three working assumptions.

1. Check Out of Politics and Ignore Its Impact on the Church.

As we talked, I realized that the wide-scale act of ignoring the election and how Trump is masterfully co-opting American Christianity is a signal of something that followers of Jesus might just need to face. It reminded me of a passage in Dederer's *Monsters* about Winifred Wagner, Richard Wagner's daughter-in-law and friend of Hitler.

"In the 1977 film *The Confessions of Winifred Wagner*, she explains that she does not care for politics, dismissively saying, 'We used to laugh about all the fuss' with a knowing smile." Dederer explains that Wagner "believes she and her kind are the ones who are free of politics, free of 'fuss.'"[7]

Here is the bigger danger of Christians opting out of the conversation about politics: We risk not just complacency but also harm compounded by the power and privilege of dusting the "fuss" of dangerous political discourse under the rug. It's a lot easier not to take politics and the danger of hate seriously when you have the privilege of averting your eyes.

2. Distance Yourself.

I believe some Christians distance ourselves from the church because we can no longer be associated with the racism-sexism-ableism-homophobia-misogyny-colonialism of white American evangelicalism. Because it is tiring to differentiate the pursuit of Jesus from a politicized version of Christianity and the church's many broken places, I have personally struggled to manage anxiety around my Christian identity and my relationship with the church. I hid the most central part of my life for the first decade-plus that I lived in Seattle, and I know where that leads. I understand how trying to keep a candle lit "under a bowl" feels (Matt. 5:15). I learned one thing from that spiritual desert: If you distance yourself from Christianity because of the broken culture around you but still try to believe, your faith is in danger of becoming unanchored. Along the way, you may let go of a beautiful, life-giving thing.

3. Vocally and Aggressively Push Back.

When you push back against messages that co-opt the Christian tradition, things are eventually asked of you—even if you are tired. When a Christian chooses this option, there is a nudge to be vocal and clear. Brave. Moral courage is required when claiming a complicated identity, but that stance can too quickly become combative and more about personal pride than Jesus.

"No," Drew said, filling my mug. "I don't think there are only three options for how Christians might live in 'Trumpified America.' Most of the brokenness in the church is from people who conflate the church with far-right politics; soon, they realize they're more interested in Trump than Jesus. Jesus will fall away. They don't need Jesus; they have Trump. He's their messiah. Look at the T-shirts."

I was dubious because Trump hadn't been elected for a second term yet. It was only early 2024, but Trump was gaining more power over evangelicalism. As we continued to talk, I began to see a fourth option—to hold fast and live faithfully. To care for "remainders"—Christians trying to hold on to faith and trying to persevere. "The 20 percent, 10 percent, or 1 percent of those who stand against Trump? We stay true. We know how to lose because Jesus lost. You either keep pressing on or you lie down and give up," Drew said.

I'm tired and feel like the holy fool, and Drew believes, against the odds. This, I have always loved about him.

I remember Isaiah 61: "He has sent me to bind up the brokenhearted, to proclaim freedom for the captives . . . to bestow on them a crown of beauty instead of ashes, the oil of joy instead of mourning, and a garment of praise instead of a spirit of despair" (vv. 1–3).

Some, like Drew, are imperfect optimists; Isaiah reminds the rest of us we're walking in faith for a reason. God's *hesed*—his steadfast love, loyal love, unfailing love—is for all of us and will make all things that are broken whole again. The spirit of despair has an answer—beauty that comes from ashes.

There will always be followers of Jesus—from every color and creed, age, sex, and geography. And those are my people. We have each other. Following are a few questions we can ask to more clearly understand the current posture of our hearts. Better to spend time thinking about these things than about what we mean by "evangelical" or "deconstructed."

Where am I motivated by anxiety, and where am I protecting myself instead of trusting God when it comes to my role in politics and the church?

Do I believe all things are being made new, even in the most broken parts of my life and culture?

Are the words I speak about other people instruments of peace, or are they tools for cutting down in order to protect and maintain my safety and power?

Can I be gentle with myself and call myself loved amid uncertainty, extending some of the compassion and loving-kindness that Christ modeled?

The names you carry within yourself are what form you. These names—forgiven, beloved, received—give you strength for the fourth option: to hold fast and live faithfully. I am convinced that even in these dark and anxious days, this is the only option that leads to true rest.

16

Holy Indifference

I didn't know much about Ignatius of Loyola except that my grandfather studied accounting at his namesake, Loyola University, in Chicago in the 1950s. I knew Loyola University had a decent basketball team, but that was about it. Later, I read that St. Ignatius was born in Basque country in the late fifteenth century and grew up to become a knight but was injured when a cannonball struck his legs during battle. In convalescence, he started a significant exploration into Jesus and the saints, was transformed, got the scruples, and went on to form the Jesuits. It wasn't until well into adulthood that I encountered any of his Spiritual Exercises.

I was dubious that a Spanish priest from the 1400s would have much to tell me today. Then, one day in 2023, I was invited by my friends Dan and Renee Huie, who co-run Soul Care Seattle, to participate in the Ignatian Spiritual Exercises, the contemplative prayer and meditation retreat first published in the mid-1500s. By "retreat," I mean daily set-apart time dedicated to the Exercises as outlined in the nineteenth annotation; the literal retreat is thirty days long, set apart and spent away. The term "annotation" is used because Ignatius outlines this modified "retreat for daily life" as the nineteenth comment in a guide for how to interact with the Exercises.

I was part of a small group that began the Exercises together—it required an hour of daily prayer for nine months instead of the month of silence. Jamie, who was in my cohort, nicknamed the retreat the "St. Iggy" and made an accompanying Spotify playlist. Many days, I prayed for closer to thirty minutes than the full hour, and I took a day or two off on weekends. It's not surprising that letting go of a scrupulous need to pray for sixty minutes a day made me feel as if I was "doing it wrong" and became a theme to pray through in my retreat.

What approximated to sixty-five hundred minutes with St. Iggy—just over one hundred hours—profoundly changed my faith. I can write without sarcasm or exaggeration that the Exercises are the best thing that ever happened to my Christian practice. I think that's in large part because throughout the nine months, instead of reading about indifference as a concept in a book, I was able to practice holy indifference in real time as my caregiving responsibilities intensified. Along the way, I wrote a "spiritual dossier"—essentially, an account of all the parts of my life, some factual and some esoteric. I was asked to include my place of birth, facial features, personality, aptitudes, hobbies, the places I lived as a kid, and more, and offer each thing to God, asking him to bless it and to care for the broken things that happened in my life. There was space in the process to consider inequity, privilege, and shame. I had time during morning prayer to turn over the nooks and crannies of my false desire and guilt. Instead of my laptop, I journaled with a pen and paper and made lists of consolations (postures toward God's love) and desolations (interior disquiet and withdrawal from God). Both recent and lifelong desolations I'd stacked in dusty corners of my mind emerged on these pages.

Retreatants were invited to use their imagination to contemplate all of creation. We were prompted to consider everything whole and broken in the world and also in our hearts—disordered thoughts or selfish actions and, as the *Book of Common Prayer* puts it, what we have done and what we have left undone.

Prayer during the retreat was like taking a highlighter through a book of my life and finding where God was a through line. It was personal, my time with St. Iggy, and completely universal to any Christian life.

Ground Rules

Ignatius wrote two collections. "The First Set of Rules" contains fourteen rules and "The Second Set of Rules" includes eight. Both sets guide participants in discernment in decisions and more so about our spiritual awareness in the whole of life. These Ignatian discernment rules simply invite awareness of our choices by noticing the root of our desire. Discernment rules in the Exercises include questions about what to do in seasons of consolation or desolation—for example, not making changes to beliefs during a bout of desolation (rule 5) and resisting temptation as early as a thought enters the mind (rule 12).[1]

The first rule of discernment notes that as Christians move from sin to sin, the enemy of our soul tempts us more. This idea was not entirely new to me. In therapy, I learned an armchair explanation for how negative patterns can be explained in the brain: If a thought occurs often enough, a channel of that thought will be carved into the mind. The trough becomes deeper over time, and it becomes harder to avoid a thought shooting down this well-worn path. When it comes to anxious, intrusive, or sinful thoughts, new neural pathways can begin to form by gently acknowledging these thoughts instead of resisting them. As I've seen in my life, time and again, resisting instead of simply noticing thoughts only makes them bigger.

Ignatius offers relief for this pattern, reminding Christians that there is help to resist well-worn thinking that leads to sin. When the enemy makes us "imagine sensual delights and pleasures," God, or "good spirit," counteracts by "pricking them and biting their consciences through the process of reason."[2]

The second discernment rule continues the thread. When Christians are "intensely cleansing their sins and rising" closer to Jesus, "it is the way of the evil spirit to bite . . . , disquieting with false reasons" to give up.[3]

I experienced this "disquiet" personally, scratching a lot of "bites" during the nine months of my retreat. I also encountered graces I savored like a piece of hard candy, moments when God came close as a counterbalance to disquiet. I began to more vividly sense how my spirit was consoled by a visual cue of something sweet: a hummingbird, the first blossom, a candle burning bright in its finger loop holder on the windowsill.

Once a week, I'd talk through notes from the previous week for an hour with Dan, my spiritual director. "Stay close to Jesus," Dan said in an early session. "Maybe put your head on his shoulder. Maybe you take a walk together. Maybe you have coffee together."

Jesus became familiar in my imagination. Sometimes in robes, sometimes in jeans and a T-shirt. When I expressed anxiety for my kid to Dan, he said, "Jesus, in his humanity, may not have known how things were going to turn out when he prayed in the garden." Sometimes, we talked about my sensing God near in afflictions. Other times, God felt far from me, and that chasm manifested as desolation. Dan told me this wasn't necessarily a bad thing. "Desolation is a drip that eventually fills up the glass," he said. This helped, because I knew enough to expect a turn back to consolation before the glass overflowed and overwhelmed—and that kept me going.

The Authentic Self Versus the False Self

Several hundred years before our wellness culture's pull to curate the authentic self to find balance, Ignatius was interested in using prayer as a tool to uncover the authentic self versus the false self through the Exercises. In *New Seeds of Contemplation*, Merton writes of his authentic self: "The secret of my identity is hidden in the love and mercy of God. But whatever is in God is really identical with Him, for His infinite simplicity admits no division and no distinction. Therefore I cannot hope to find myself anywhere except in Him."[4]

There's no formula or "right" way to go about the process of discerning the true and false self. It doesn't require spending money on a retreat or formal theological training.

Here is what happens to many people, in no particular order, through discernment during the Exercises: You learn how to listen more than talk in prayer. You begin to more deeply believe God is loving and you in particular are loved. Your eyes are open to your depravity in new ways. By articulating the qualities of your authentic self, you can more freely practice indifference to the outcomes in your life.

In my case, I prayed, listened, and still struggled to name much of my authentic self in the first months of the Exercises. I found soft answers without difficulty, but they were focused on what I do more than who I am: listens to music; just like St. Francis, loves animals; notices seasons: berries growing in the backyard, winter blooms. When I went much deeper, discerning who I "really am" as a child of God was harder and began to sound aspirational, an image of who I'd like to be rather than who I am: faithful to friends, long-suffering. Really, what's true is that I try to be faithful and would like to be long-suffering.

On the other hand, it was easy for me to list messages I've intuited about my false self. I'm floaty and awkward. I'm "too much" for friends. I don't know how to relate to women. It's hard to get to know me, and that, at times, is a point of pride. I'm too sarcastic. I'm cranky when I'm tired. I prove my worth through productivity. My ego easily rises and falls. I am anxious, both genetically and in how I was raised, and I can never escape its grip. See? Easy.

One day, I made a note of something Dan said in a session to remember it: "Don't judge your false self because God doesn't judge it but works to transform it." If we can be spiritually free to notice and expect the false self, the authentic self begins to surface.

What Indifference Is (and Isn't)

In the Spiritual Exercises, Ignatius teaches that humans are made to praise and serve God and that the earth was created for people to revere God and find salvation. This central "principle and foundation" is built around the idea that *all is gift*. As spiritual director Dale Gish writes in his modern translation of the Exercises, "All we have and the details of our life are gifts from God, given to help us pursue the purpose for which we are created" so that we can "embrace these things, in so far as they help us toward our purpose, and free ourselves from them, in so far as they are obstacles to our purpose. We are invited to learn holy indifference to the particular circumstances of our life so that we can seek God and God's kingdom above all else."[5]

Detachment or indifference outside of the Ignatian context may sound like permission to care less or check out. But as Gish clarifies, "For Ignatius, indifference is not about being detached, resignation, fatalism or the absence of desire. . . . Holy indifference is not a state where we do not care about what happens; instead, it is a state of true love."[6]

Holy indifference is not about trying to wrangle God's will around a preferred, less anxious outcome. Instead, indifference leads to a state of peace with any outcome if it's in God's good order. "Indifference means being detached enough from things, people, or experiences to be able either to take them up or to leave them aside, depending on whether they help us 'to praise, reverence, and serve God' (*Spiritual Exercises* 23)," Boston College philosophy professor Marina McCoy explains. "In other words, it's the capacity to let go of what doesn't help me to love God or love others—*while staying engaged with what does*."[7]

Practicing holy indifference brings us closer to spiritual freedom, which releases us from striving "to be single or married, to have power or no power, work in this job or that one, to be a leader or serve behind the scenes, to live in the city or the country, and any other circumstance."[8] Joined with spiritual disciplines, such as prayer and fasting, indifference is an important tool to move you closer to your true self, to who you are.

Practicing Holy Indifference

Saint Ignatius lays out a series of binaries to achieve indifference around: "Thus for our part we should not want health more than sickness, wealth more than poverty, fame more than disgrace, a long life more than a short one—and so with everything else; desiring and choosing only what leads more to the end for which we are created."[9]

For each of these binaries, there is tension between our full desire and our full acceptance. That overlap is where God meets us as we become indifferent to any outcome. For example, I can fully desire to restore a broken relationship with a friend. And, the best I'm able, I can accept that the relationship could remain broken. In the gap is where I can discern, listen in prayer, and find direction. Praying that God would bring you to indifference about any outcome lets you more deeply long for restoration—and more fully accept the possibility that healing or reconciliation may not be found. Slowly, the outcome of our prayer becomes less central to our need to be near God.

I've prayed for Asher's OCD while in various emotional states: with a sense of peace, in a state of despair, on the floor in the kitchen the morning when we knew something was wrong but didn't know what it was, in the middle of the night during an emotional hangover after a difficult day. I've prayed for him with other people, over him while he slept, by his side in church.

It was while doing the Exercises that I tried for the first time to bring a posture of holy indifference to my kid's circumstances. One morning, I woke up before anyone else, lit a candle, and went out on the porch. I asked God to be near and sat in silence for several minutes until I sensed God's love, close and quiet. I imagined Asher standing with Jesus, and I prayed that whether his life is easy or difficult, breezy or afflicted, whether he is surrounded by a community or lonely, found or lost, God's love would remain near.

I prayed that God would feel the actual feelings of hope and fear for my kid that I did—in the stomach. Then I released the need to control my son's outcomes and gave him to God. I imagined sending control up in the air like a paper lantern and opened my eyes.

Kathleen Norris calls detachment "the ability to live at peace with the reality of whatever happens. Such people do not have a closed-off air, nor a boastful demeanor. In them, it is clear, their wounds have opened the way to compassion for others. And compassion is the strength and soul of a religion."[10] We bring dignity to ourselves and other people through building a deeper understanding of our longings.

Norris says, "This sort of detachment is neither passive nor remote but paradoxically is fully engaged with the world."[11]

At that moment on the porch, this is very much how I felt. Near to my son, mothering my son, and accepting a future for him I can't predict. I simply knew that he is loved by God and by me and that height or depth can't shake it.

Cloud-Shadows and Dry Woods

In her essay *Detachment*, Simone Weil says, "We must give up everything which is not grace and not even desire grace."[12] When I first read this, I felt like a big baby. I hadn't really noticed grace enough in my own life to desire or stop desiring.

I remember myself clearly, age twenty-one, reading Weil for the first time at a study-in-the-mountains semester in southern Oregon. I read her essays out loud and tried to understand them.

After reading Weil, I walked up and down the little mountain highway and spoke out loud Rilke's poems to better be present to them. "So you mustn't be frightened, if a sadness rises in front of you, larger than any you have ever seen; if an anxiety, like light and cloud-shadows, moves over your hands and over everything you do,"[13] Rilke writes in *Letters to a Young Poet*, a book that every female college English major thinks is about her. She is kind of right.

That semester, in the dry woods outside of Ashland with Dostoevsky, David James Duncan, Rilke, and Weil, I lived with a sense of boundlessness that didn't seem to need holy indifference. Weil's detachment was interesting to me, a piece of sunstone from eastern Oregon to hold and turn to catch different angles of light. In those optimistic and shielded years, tarantulas, scorpions, and snakes did not lurk but rather sunned themselves on the dry dirt. I would read Weil and Rilke without watching my step.

Reading Weil half a life later, benefitting from the privilege of health insurance and a new roof overhead in a house with a view of downtown Seattle from the kitchen sink, I wonder if I am closer or further from understanding true detachment. Was I closer to holy indifference as a college student because I was less tethered to stuff? Was the optimism of youth the closest I'd ever be to full freedom? I benefited from blind spots then, but sooner or later I'd have to open my eyes to the indifference that is only understood in the context of trial.

I wondered for a long time about the equity of indifference. My parents footed the bill for my semester in Ashland. To be fair, Ignatius would not have applied the term "access" to indifference or talked about the privilege around it like we do today. But *come on*, I think. Is a migrant family trying to cross the border supposed to be holding a posture of indifference? Are people who are unhoused in downtown Seattle able to be indifferent about their safety and well-being? Should they be?

Applying indifference to whether we have "power or no power" is easier as a hypothetical. It can be hard to see how justice and indifference interact. Action is involved in justice, while indifference is inward work. Even though they seem like opposite postures, I'm convinced that indifference is the foundation of care. It may seem counterintuitive, but we can't fully care or be cared for if we don't believe God's kingdom will one day right every injustice. Indifference allows us to accept the larger story.

In the last reflection in the Exercises, called the "Contemplation of Divine Love," Ignatius shares two key ideas. First, Christians express our love to God not just by what we say but also by what we do, by the actions we take or choose not to take. Second, love is relational. Even in the presence of evil, we can commit to one another while God works for good to bring creation to redemption.[14]

Not long ago, I was messaging with my friend Yising about whether privilege is necessarily embedded in Ignatian indifference. "I believe holy indifference is core to the Sermon on the Mount," Yising texted me. "Jesus knew he would be crucified by the empire he was choosing not to overthrow in the moment—and that many of his followers would be martyred by the same empire—but he still said not to worry."

Holy indifference manifests acutely in the night garden, where Jesus prays, "Father, if you are willing, take this cup from me; yet not my will, but yours be done" (Luke 22:42). The outcome of Jesus's life is ultimately important—his death for our life. But it's also important to consider his posture of complete acceptance in a time of uncertainty. To make the choice to pray "not my will, but yours be done" required Jesus to fully trust in his Father's goodness. Jesus does not turn, resist, or force his will when the cup of affliction and death is not removed. Jesus suffers for a good reason: he is settled in God's love.

"Not my will, but yours be done." When Jesus teaches his followers to pray using the Lord's Prayer, he is taking a posture of holy indifference or detachment. I wonder if in the act of God the Father letting Jesus the Son be martyred, he was modeling indifference too.

Truthfully, "will" has generally negative connotations for me. Will is force; it is pushing against. It is athletic, active. Will is pulling yourself up by your bootstraps. Will reminds me of the free will/determinism debates around Calvinism and Arminianism—armchair predestination fights I'm not interested in having. I associate "will" with a lot of things, but none of them are light or airy. My own will is something I press against, wrestle with. But holy indifference manifests with a light touch. It's a kind of submission that draws you near to God.

Holy indifference is a relief. When Christians are indifferent to any outcome, we model to each other conviction anchored to hope. We can resist oppression and work for justice because it's the right thing to do regardless of whether we have a fighting chance. We can resist and lose and not be overcome or anxious.

We're each here for a little while, and hopefully we love and are loved. People may remember us, or we may be forgotten. Our bodies may be eaten by cancer or be perfectly healthy. We may die in childhood, die in war, or die of old age during a Sunday afternoon nap.

God knows you intricately, just as he does everybody else. You are completely known and loved in the irreplaceable complexity of your life.

Once in a spiritual direction session, Dan said, "God is the flame of love burning in every created thing." Be it in health or sickness, wealth or poverty, fame or disgrace, a long life or a short life, holy indifference reveals to us love burning in all of creation. Holy indifference helps us make peace with this truth: we don't control much. Bad things will continue to come and so will joy. Everything is completely broken, and extraordinarily there is hope: my anxious mind at rest, my mother's body in motion, my father's cancer swallowed whole, the church's evil erased, broken hearts mended, empires reduced to the rule of a tenderhearted God.

Anxious, Not Afraid

Why are we anxious about our bodies and the bodies of people we love? Because our bodies are disconnected from healthy desire and failed by the promise of wellness. Embodiment grounds us from the inside out. Why are we anxious about the church body? Because the church has absorbed anxiety instead of bearing peace. Becoming a nonanxious presence welcomes a flourishing community. Why are we anxious about the body politic? Because politics and culture wars bind our well-being to outcomes. Holy indifference frees.

If Jesus said to not worry, I believe he meant it. The pain point—the dissonance between the head reading "do not worry" and the heart worrying—was the one I began to understand through embodiment, stability, fidelity, and nonanxious presence that ultimately led me to embrace a posture of holy indifference. I think about indifference every day. It is a companion with me on the journey, truly nourishing and helpful in small and major personal, church, and political trials.

I've wanted to find a cooler or refresher, a tonic to quench my anxiety. I've hung my head over the kitchen butcher block, praying for healing for my anxiety. I've laid on the bathroom floor under the window at night, asking for relief from my anxiety, but it has not left me. The moonlight is a different kind of light. I'm still anxious, but I am not afraid; rather, I am increasingly openhanded. God did not take away my anxiety. Instead, God met me in my anxiety by helping me to become indifferent to it.

Epilogue

Last night Dad called at 3:00 a.m. Mom was frozen in bed, her Parkinson's flaring. Can I come, help lift her to the toilet and calm her down so she can sleep? Driving over, I heard a BBC report about a Russian missile that killed thirty-four people at a children's hospital in Ukraine. The suffering, near and far, is too much.

Driving home from my parents' place, I remembered something that happened during my recent trip to Michigan. I'd woken up heavy with anxiety during the last morning of a writing conference in Grand Rapids. I made a mug of coffee and walked to an old Catholic cemetery across from the house I was staying in with friends.

The sun is rising as I move toward old graves, one marked by a statue of Mary with the sacred heart, her hands open. A mother when I need to be mothered. I walk up a hill toward a grove of pine trees. I have spent so much time thinking about death and have wanted so much to live free of the anxiety of these years. I want to live while I am alive. I am forty-six years old.

I put on headphones and listen to the John Prine song "Summer's End." It makes me weep for the first time in months. The song reminds me of a dear man, also named John, a pastor from Kentucky in my writing program. He'd read in tears to a group of us: "My sadness is born of love." John said his dad used to take him out in the middle of the night to listen to the corn grow. I go to the old graves and think of sad love, of listening love.

I find a set of graves with a family's surname on a stone in the center among a cluster of stones that say "Father," "Mother," and the names of their children, Josephine and Clarence. I see a grave marked with the image of a palm, another with an olive branch. At others, there are small stone crosses tilted against gravestones covered in flowers. I remember that Jesus was buried in a garden tomb.

Then, looking to the end of the graves—a deer: huge, standing so still I wonder if she is a statue. The deer, surefooted and steady. I move closer as she begins to leap over the graves. All these people, these friendships and loves, had their season and are gone, and life is moving over them. Slender feet, a gallop, a sort of dance. God, dancing over death. Death is not the end. I turn the thought over and over in my mind, like a piece of hard candy in my mouth, and it is sweet. God, showing me life in the presence of death.

The Spiritual Exercises ended a few months later in May of 2024, the night before the northern lights swept across a lot of the US. They were seen on the West Coast and the East Coast, all the way down to my friend's porch in Arkansas. Our family met neighbors in Seattle and walked to a park down the street with a field carved out like a fruit bowl.

We waited, and for a long time nothing happened. Then we thought we saw something: looking through the phone screen, a little green, a streak of red. Standing up, I turned with my phone in a circle in the fruit bowl field with dozens of neighbors, surrounded by falling color. I looked up until my neck hurt and then laid down on a blanket we'd brought along where my daughter had fallen asleep. She woke up for a moment and saw the sky. "I'm so happy, Mama."

After arriving home past midnight, I stood on the back porch and saw the red aurora through dark pink camellia blossoms. Another night garden. I thought of the psalmist, writing in times of lament and joy: "His love has taken over our lives" (Ps. 117:2 MSG). Suffering, grief, and affliction are long seasons, but they will not last forever. The love of God gifts us with moments of light. Right then, down to the wire, I believe Ignatius: everything is gift.

I stand for a few minutes in the dark and think again of the deer, the graveyard. My parents sleeping, the kids sleeping, and the house at rest. Red flowers in violent bloom. In the presence of little hells, and actual hell, yes, that's it: there is life.

Acknowledgments

Thank you to my agent, John Blase, and Stephanie Duncan Smith, who acquired this book.

Thanks to the whole Baker Books team, including Eddie LaRow, Shelly MacNaughton, Gisèle Mix, Olivia Peitsch, and Robin Turici. Thanks to developmental editor (and fellow Pacific Northwesterner) Shari MacDonald Strong and publicist Kelly Hughes. Many thanks to cover designer Jake Nicolella: lilies growing out of an anxious mind? I'm seriously considering a tattoo.

Thanks to *Bitter Scroll* readers and *That's the Spirit* listeners. Thanks to the Kindred Collective, mashing up friendship and writing in the middle of Kentucky every February, especially to Winn Collier for seeing something in my writing years ago when I couldn't. To the Cairns, of course: Amber Haines, Jessica Herberger, and Lore Ferguson Wilbert.

Thanks to the Grace Seattle Vestry and staff: Jamie Afshari, Jess Alldredge, Nate Andrews, Eric Hadden, Nelson and Nicole Hall, John and Linn Haralson, Rebecca Ifland,

and Darik Taniguchi. Dan and Renee Huie, thank you for leading me through the Exercises, which changed everything. Special thanks to Tamarack Randall, who let me edit chapters in her apartment—stocked with popcorn and Lillet—while she was traveling.

Thanks to the many friends who have rooted for this book, including Keren Baltzer, Lisa Behringer, Joshua Bocanegra, Drew Brown, Yi Ning Chiu, Yising Chou, Kris Cysyk, Chuck DeGroat, Janell Downing, Sara Eagan, Jon and Val Guerra, Josh Jeter, John Leggett, Marilyn McEntyre, Kevin and Jessica Schlereth, Chris Smith, Amanda Uhle, and Sarah Westfall.

A special thanks to Morgan Page, whose friendship and creative partnership have been a total pleasure.

Dad, you've become the most unlikely, and most wonderful, caregiver. I'm proud to be your kid.

Mom, in all you're walking through, you've remained hopeful and faithful. Always loving you.

Sabine, you're confetti, sparklers, cake with ice cream. Where would we be without the loving-kindness you bring?

Asher, you are bright and clear-eyed. I love who you are and who you're becoming.

Drew, thank you for believing in this book and walking by my side. You're faithful, hopeful, and long-suffering. Being our family's nonanxious presence? You're a natural.

Notes

Introduction

1. Christine Runyan, "On Healing Our Distressed Nervous Systems," interview by Krista Tippett, *On Being*, last updated May 30, 2024, https://onbeing.org/programs/christine-runyan-on-healing-our-distressed-nervous-systems/#transcript.

2. Mark Sayers, *A Non-Anxious Presence: How a Changing and Complex World Will Create a Remnant of Renewed Christian Leaders* (Moody Publishers, 2022), 37.

3. Sayers, *A Non-Anxious Presence*, 37.

4. Sayers, *A Non-Anxious Presence*, 38.

5. Nick Cave, "Loss, Yearning, Transcendence," interview by Krista Tippett, *On Being*, last updated November 22, 2023, https://onbeing.org/programs/nick-cave-loss-yearning-transcendence/.

6. Sofia Onte, "The Truth Is I'm Tired, But I'm Still Fighting," Thought.is, accessed November 25, 2024, https://thought.is/the-truth-is-im-tired-but-im-still-fighting/.

7. Thierry Steimer, "The Biology of Fear- and Anxiety-Related Behaviors," *Dialogues in Clinical Neuroscience* 4, no. 3 (September 2002): 231–49, https://pmc.ncbi.nlm.nih.gov/articles/PMC3181681/.

8. Steimer, "Biology of Fear- and Anxiety-Related Behaviors."

9. "Mental Health Today: A Deep Dive Based on the 2023 Gen Z and Millennial Survey," Deloitte, May 2023, https://www2.deloitte.com/content/dam/Deloitte/global/Documents/deloitte-2023-genz-millennial-survey-mental-health.pdf.

10. Walton Family Foundation, *Voices of Gen Z: Perspectives on U.S. Education, Wellbeing and the Future* (Gallup, 2023), 3, https://nextgeninsights.waltonfamilyfoundation.org/resources/wff-and-gallup-gen-z-panel/.

11. Sayers, *A Non-Anxious Presence*, 191.

12. Russell Moore, host, *The Russell Moore Show*, podcast, episode 90, "Kate Bowler Tells Us Where We're Wrong on Suffering," *Christianity Today*, January 31, 2024, https://www.christianitytoday.com/podcasts/the-russell-moore-show/kate-bowler-tells-us-where-were-wrong-on-suffering/.

Chapter 1 Leans Anxious

1. "Anxiety Disorders—Facts & Statistics," Anxiety and Depression Association of America, accessed November 25, 2024, https://adaa.org/understanding-anxiety/facts-statistics#Facts%20and%20Statistics.

2. *Lucky Hank*, season 1, episode 1, "Pilot," directed by Peter Farrelly, aired March 19, 2023, on AMC, https://www.amcplus.com/pages/lucky-hank.

3. "What's Normal Anxiety—and What's An Anxiety Disorder?," YouTube video, posted by TED, July 1, 2021, https://www.youtube.com/watch?app=desktop&v=xsEJ6GeAGb0.

4. Matthew S. Boone, Jennifer A. Gregg, and Lisa W. Coyne, "You Are Not Your Thoughts," *Psychology Today*, April 14, 2022, https://www.psychologytoday.com/us/blog/stop-avoiding-stuff/202204/you-are-not-your-thoughts#:~:text=Remind%20yourself%20that%20you%20are,as%20if%20from%20a%20distance.

5. Boone, Gregg, and Coyne, "You Are Not Your Thoughts."

Chapter 2 Anxious Bodies

1. Runyan, "On Healing Our Distressed Nervous Systems."

2. Frederick Buechner, *Now and Then: A Memoir of Vocation* (HarperSanFrancisco, 1983), 61.

3. Buechner, *Now and Then*, 63.

4. "Prayers for Deliverance and Healing," *The Catholic Company*, accessed November 25, 2024, https://www.catholiccompany.com/content/prayers-for-deliverance-and-healing.

5. Agnes Sanford, *The Healing Light* (Harper & Row, 1967), 35.

6. Sanford, *The Healing Light*, 31.

7. Dennis Bennett, *Nine O'Clock in the Morning* (Harper & Row, 1970), 100.

8. Sanford, *The Healing Light*, 31.

9. Sanford, *The Healing Light*, 38.

10. "Epigenetics and Child Development: How Children's Experiences Affect Their Genes," Center on the Developing Child, February 19, 2019, https://developingchild.harvard.edu/resources/what-is-epigenetics-and-how-does-it-relate-to-child-development/#:~:text=%E2%80%9CEpigenetics%E2%80%9D%20is%20an%20emerging%20area,is%20no%20longer%20a%20debate.

11. Tori Rodriguez, "Descendants of Holocaust Survivors Have Altered Stress Hormones," *Scientific American*, March 1, 2015, https://www.scientificamerican.com/article/descendants-of-holocaust-survivors-have-altered-stress-hormones/.

12. Madison Margolin, "Why Jewish Anxiety Is No Laughing Matter," *Forward*, August 9, 2015, https://forward.com/culture/318509/is-jewish-anxiety-no-laughing-matter/.

Chapter 3 Path of Wellness

1. Rachel Tashjian, "A Mordant Glimpse at the Austrian Aristocracy," *T Magazine*, October 5, 2023, https://www.nytimes.com/2023/10/05/t-magazine/victoria-hely-hutchinson-photography.html.
2. Hemlock Neversink, Foster Supply Hospitality, accessed November 25, 2024, https://www.hemlockneversink.com/.
3. Hemlock Neversink.
4. Hemlock Neversink.
5. Tashjian, "A Mordant Glimpse."
6. Tashjian, "A Mordant Glimpse."
7. Jessica DeFino, "Eat Me!," *The Review of Beauty by Jessica DeFino* (blog), October 8, 2023, https://jessicadefino.substack.com/p/dewy-dumpling-skin.
8. Jessica DeFino, "The Rise and Rise of 'Dewy Dumpling Skin,'" *Sunday Times*, October 8, 2023, https://www.thetimes.com/life-style/beauty/article/the-rise-and-rise-of-dewy-dumpling-skin-v9mwk2qzc.
9. DeFino, "Rise and Rise of 'Dewy Dumpling Skin.'"
10. Anne Lamott, "It's Good to Remember: We Are All on Borrowed Time," *Washington Post*, October 30, 2023, https://www.washingtonpost.com/opinions/2023/10/30/aging-health-strength-mind-heart/.

Chapter 4 Sundowning

1. "Beth Becomes Sick - 'Little Women' - Winona Ryder, Claire Danes," YouTube video, posted by Veronique Laurent, January 27, 2017, https://www.youtube.com/watch?v=aDRr3HvzrrE.
2. Joan Didion, *Blue Nights* (Alfred A. Knopf, 2011), 4.
3. Claire Dederer, *Monsters: A Fan's Dilemma* (Doubleday, 2023).
4. Sherwood Anderson, *Winesburg, Ohio* (Boni & Liveright, 1919), 1.
5. Anderson, *Winesburg, Ohio*, 5.
6. Kathleen Norris, interview by Bob Abernethy, *Religion & Ethics NewsWeekly*, PBS, March 13, 2009, https://www.pbs.org/wnet/religionandethics/2009/03/13/march-13-2009-kathleen-norris/1343/.
7. Norris, interview.
8. Norris, interview.

Chapter 5 Hotel Corazón

1. Yuan Spa, "Hydrotherapy," accessed November 18, 2023, https://yuanspa.com/hydrotherapy/.
2. Classical King FM, *Evenings with Peter Newman*, July 28, 2023.

3. Amy Tara Koch, "Hotel Corazón Wants to Host Your Hot Girl Summer," *New York Times*, June 22, 2023, https://www.nytimes.com/2023/06/22/style/hotel-corazon-majorca-spain.html.

4. Hotel Corazón, accessed December 1, 2023, https://www.hotelcorazon.com/.

5. "Dementia," Parkinson's Foundation, accessed March 21, 2025, https://www.parkinson.org/understanding-parkinsons/non-movement-symptoms/dementia.

6. *BibleProject Podcast*, Character of God series, episode 3, "*The Womb of God?*," August 31, 2020, https://bibleproject.com/podcast/the-womb-of-god/.

Chapter 6 Caregiving

1. *Julia*, season 1, episode 3, "Beef Bourguignon," directed by Melanie Mayron, aired March 31, 2022, on HBO.

Chapter 7 Embodiment

1. Anna Harris, "Embodiment," *Oxford Bibliographies*, last updated August 30, 2016, https://www.oxfordbibliographies.com/display/document/obo-9780199766567/obo-9780199766567-0151.xml#:~:text=Although%20the%20concept%20becomes%20different,in%20and%20with%20inhabited%20worlds.

2. Bishop Todd Hunter, host, *The C4SO Podcast*, "David Taylor on Body & Worship," The Diocese of Churches for the Sake of Others, June 13, 2023, https://c4so.org/podcast/david-taylor-on-body-worship/.

3. Hillary L. McBride, *The Wisdom of Your Body: Finding Healing, Wholeness, and Connection through Embodied Living* (Brazos Press, 2021), 12, 25.

4. McBride, *Wisdom of Your Body*, 13.

5. McBride, *Wisdom of Your Body*, 24.

6. Katy Butler, *The Art of Dying Well: A Practical Guide to a Good End of Life* (Scribner, 2020).

7. Daria Mitiuk, Constant Méheut, and Laura Boushnak, "Grieving Ukrainians Turn to 'Death Doulas' for Support," *New York Times*, July 24, 2024, https://www.nytimes.com/2024/07/24/world/europe/ukraine-death-doula-russia-war.html.

8. *Book of Common Prayer* (The Episcopal Church, 1979), 101, Wikisource, last edited May 23, 2022, https://en.wikisource.org/wiki/Page:Book_of_common_prayer_(TEC,_1979).pdf/101.

9. Dallas Willard, "Spiritual Formation and the Warfare Between the Flesh and the Human Spirit," Conversatio Divina, accessed November 27, 2024, https://conversatio.org/spiritual-formation-and-the-warfare-between-the-flesh-and-the-human-spirit/.

10. Tsh Oxenreider, host, *A Drink with a Friend*, podcast, episode 160, "Flourishing and Acedia," February 9, 2024, https://thecommon.place/p/ep160.

11. Hunter, "David Taylor on Body & Worship."

12. Hunter, "David Taylor on Body & Worship."

13. "A Morning Prayer Written by St. Therese," *EWTN*, accessed November 26, 2024, https://www.ewtn.com/catholicism/devotions/morning-prayer-written-by-st-therese-838.

Chapter 8 Scrupulosity

1. US Surgeon General's Advisory, "Our Epidemic of Loneliness and Isolation" (US Department of Health and Human Services, 2023), https://www.hhs.gov/sites/default/files/surgeon-general-social-connection-advisory.pdf.

2. Jonathan Haidt, "End the Phone-Based Childhood Now," *Atlantic*, March 13, 2024, https://www.theatlantic.com/technology/archive/2024/03/teen-childhood-smartphone-use-mental-health-effects/677722/.

3. Haidt, "End the Phone-Based Childhood Now."

4. Haidt, "End the Phone-Based Childhood Now."

5. Russell Moore, host, *The Russell Moore Show*, podcast, episode 100, "An Update to The Anxious Generation with Jonathan Haidt," *Christianity Today*, April 3, 2024, https://www.russellmoore.com/2024/04/03/an-update-to-the-anxious-generation-with-jonathan-haidt/.

6. Andrew Rosen, "What Is Religious OCD?," Center for Treatment of Anxiety and Mood Disorders, accessed November 26, 2024, https://centerforanxietydisorders.com/what-is-religious-ocd/#:~:text=People%20with%20religious%20OCD%20strongly,within%20very%20strict%20religious%20cultures.

7. Frederick Buechner, *Telling Secrets* (HarperSanFrancisco, 1991), 26.

8. Buechner, *Telling Secrets*, 26.

9. Emily Palmer et al., "Preventing Anxiety in the Children of Anxious Parents—Feasibility of a Brief, Online, Group Intervention for Parents of One- to Three-Year-Olds," *Child and Adolescent Mental Health* 28, no. 1 (2023): 33–41, https://acamh.onlinelibrary.wiley.com/doi/pdf/10.1111/camh.12596.

10. Sara Anderson, "Atheism Scrupulosity," NOCD, October 25, 2022, https://www.treatmyocd.com/what-is-ocd/common-fears/fear-of-atheism-ocd.

11. Klindt's Booksellers, "John Bunyan, *Visions of Heaven and Hell* (paperback)," accessed November 26, 2024, https://www.klindtsbooks.com/book/9781499525335.

12. Luke Lancaster, "The Scruples of Luther and Thérèse," Catholic Answers, June 1, 2021, https://www.catholic.com/magazine/online-edition/the-scruples-of-luther-and-therese.

13. R. C. Sproul, "Was Luther Insane?," Tabletalk, October 28, 2024, https://tabletalkmagazine.com/posts/was-luther-insane/#:~:text=But%20even%20that%20moment%20isn,to%20go%20through%20daily%20confession.

14. Amanda Knapp, "The Two Saints Who Saved Me from Scrupulosity," America: The Jesuit Review, July 27, 2022, https://www.americamagazine.org/faith/2022/07/27/saint-ignatius-scruples-sin-243314.

15. "Chapter Nine: Some Notes Concerning Scruples," My Catholic Life!, accessed March 31, 2025, https://mycatholic.life/books/ignatius/part-one-back

ground-of-saint-ignatius-and-lessons-from-the-spiritual-exercises/chapter-nine-some-notes-concerning-scruples/.

16. "Chapter Nine: Some Notes Concerning Scruples."

17. Paulina Albińska, "Scrupulosity–Cognitive-Behavioural Understanding of Religious/Moral Obsessive-Compulsive Disorder" Psychiatr Psychol Klin, April 29, 2022, https://www.psychiatria.com.pl/assets/pdf/artykuly/25-39-pipk-1-2022-albinska.pdf.

18. Joan Didion, *The Year of Magical Thinking* (Alfred A. Knopf, 2005), 32–33.

Chapter 9 Stability

1. Willie James Jennings, *The Christian Imagination: Theology and the Origins of Race* (Yale University Press, 2010), 248.

2. Jennings, *The Christian Imagination*, 248.

3. W. David O. Taylor, *A Body of Praise: Understanding the Role of Our Physical Bodies in Worship* (Baker Academic, 2023), 4.

4. "What We Learned About the Embodied Church During the Pandemic," *Christianity Today*, March 2021, https://www.christianitytoday.com/scot-mcknight/2021/march/what-we-learned-about-embodied-church-during-pandemic.html (article discontinued).

5. Lia Eustachewich, "How the Seattle CHOP Zone Went from Socialist Summer Camp to Deadly Disaster," *New York Post*, July 1, 2020, https://nypost.com/2020/07/01/how-seattle-chop-went-from-socialist-summer-camp-to-deadly-disaster/.

6. Dyer Oxley and David Hyde, "Shattered Windows and Nerves, Seattle's Wing Luke Museum Targeted in Alleged Hate Crime," KUOW, September 15, 2023, https://www.kuow.org/stories/shattered-windows-and-nerves-seattle-s-wing-luke-museum-targeted-in-alleged-hate-crime.

7. Bishop Todd Hunter, host, *The C4SO Podcast*, "Winn Collier on Ordinary Time," The Diocese of Churches for the Sake of Others, February 7, 2024, https://c4so.org/podcast/winn-collier-on-ordinary-time/.

8. Hunter, "Winn Collier on Ordinary Time."

Chapter 10 Fidelity

1. "Conversatio Morum," *Oblate Spring* (blog), accessed November 26, 2024, https://www.oblatespring.com/oblatespring0202conversatio.htm.

2. "Vow of Fidelity to the Monastic Way of Life," Sisters of St. Benedict, April 21, 2023, https://thedome.org/vow-of-fidelity/#:~:text=Vow%20of%20Fidelity%20to%20the%20Monastic%20Way%20of%20Life&text=This%20vow%20allows%20us%20to,us%20on%20the%20island%20alone.&text=The%20Sisters%20of%20St.,the%20extent%20allowed%20by%20law.

3. Marilynne Robinson, *What Are We Doing Here? Essays* (Farrar, Straus and Giroux, 2018), 35.

4. Robinson, *What Are We Doing Here?*, 36.
5. Robinson, *What Are We Doing Here?*, 37.
6. Miroslav Volf, *Exclusion and Embrace: A Theological Exploration of Identity, Otherness, and Reconciliation* (Abingdon, 2019).
7. Lesslie Newbigin, *The Household of God: Lectures on the Nature of the Church* (SCM Press, 1953), 56.
8. Newbigin, *Household of God*, 29.
9. Kathleen Norris, *Amazing Grace: A Vocabulary of Faith* (Riverhead Books, 1998), 273.
10. Chuck DeGroat (@ChuckDeGroat), "Where trust is low and anxiety is high within a church or Christian org," Instagram, April 16, 2024, https://www.instagram.com/chuckdegroat/p/C50uQmKLnzU/.
11. DeGroat, "Where trust is low."
12. Newbigin, *Household of God*, 132.

Chapter 11 Energy Vampires

1. Jancee Dunn, "The 6-Day Energy Challenge," *New York Times*, January 1, 2024, https://www.nytimes.com/explain/2024/energy-challenge#energy-challenge-friendship.
2. Dunn, "6-Day Energy Challenge."
3. Dunn, "6-Day Energy Challenge."
4. Anna Medaris, "Feeling Drained from the Night Before? It Could Be an Emotional Hangover," *Vox*, July 21, 2024, https://www.vox.com/24119926/emotional-hangover-fights-feelings-how-to-handle.
5. Thomas Merton and Sue Monk Kidd, *New Seeds of Contemplation* (New Directions, 2007), 36.
6. Constance Grady, "When You Can't Separate Art from Artist," *Vox*, June 22, 2023, https://www.vox.com/the-gray-area/23768672/claire-dederer-interview-monsters-a-fans-dilemma-me-too.
7. Grady, "When You Can't Separate Art from Artist."
8. Norris, *Amazing Grace*, 14.

Chapter 12 Religious but Not Spiritual

1. Fleming Rutledge, *Three Hours: Sermons for Good Friday* (Eerdmans, 2019), 10.
2. Sally Rooney, *Beautiful World, Where Are You* (Picador, 2022), 194.
3. Cave, "Loss, Yearning, Transcendence."
4. Cave, "Loss, Yearning, Transcendence."
5. Eugene Peterson, "Answering God," interview by Krista Tippett, *On Being*, last updated April 7, 2022, https://onbeing.org/programs/eugene-peterson-answering-god/.
6. Rick Rubin, host, *Tetragrammaton with Rick Rubin*, podcast, "Nick Cave," November 15, 2023, https://open.spotify.com/episode/7yT6GVkOVebVlOsqdHRYwK?si=3p7jWhD5Ta2u4JaA8cUdeA.

7. Edwin H. Friedman, Margaret M. Treadwell, and Edward W. Beal, *A Failure of Nerve: Leadership in the Age of the Quick Fix* (Seabury Books, 2007), 59.

8. Sayers, *A Non-Anxious Presence*, 42.

Chapter 13 Political Anxiety

1. Danny E. Olinger, "Geerhardus Vos: Family Life, the Kingdom of God, and the Church," *Ordained Servant Online*, April 2017, accessed November 26, 2024, https://opc.org/os.html?article_id=620.

2. Russell Moore, host, *The Russell Moore Show*, podcast, episode 107, "Predictions About the Future of the Christian Church," *Christianity Today*, May 22, 2024, https://www.christianitytoday.com/podcasts/the-russell-moore-show/predictions-future-of-christian-church-evangelicalism/.

3. "Political Anxiety," *Good Therapy* (blog), last updated May 18, 2017, https://www.goodtherapy.org/blog/psychpedia/political-anxiety.

4. "2020 Presidential Election a Source of Significant Stress for More Americans Than 2016 Presidential Race," American Psychological Association, October 7, 2020, https://www.apa.org/news/press/releases/2020/10/election-stress.

5. Tim Reid, "Trump Tells Christians They Won't Have to Vote After This Election," *Reuters*, July 28, 2024, https://www.reuters.com/world/us/trump-tells-christians-they-wont-have-vote-after-this-election-2024-07-27/.

6. Nellie Bowles, "Louisiana Requires All Public Classrooms to Display Ten Commandments," *New York Times*, June 19, 2024, https://www.nytimes.com/2024/06/19/us/louisiana-ten-commandments-classrooms.html.

7. Mary Whitfill Roeloffs, "Trump Loves 'Ten Commandments in Public Schools': Says Louisiana Law Could Be 'Major Step' in Religion Revival," *Forbes*, June 21, 2024, https://www.forbes.com/sites/maryroeloffs/2024/06/21/louisianas-new-ten-commandments-law-is-latest-example-of-states-pushing-to-allow-religion-in-public-schools/.

8. "Religious Pluralism 101," Aspen Institute, July 17, 2019, https://www.aspeninstitute.org/blog-posts/religious-pluralism-101/#:~:text=Religious%20pluralism%20is%20the%20state,as%20one%20out%20of%20many.

9. "45% of Americans Say U.S. Should Be a 'Christian Nation,'" Pew Research Center, October 27, 2022, https://www.pewresearch.org/religion/2022/10/27/45-of-americans-say-u-s-should-be-a-christian-nation/.

10. *Merriam-Webster Dictionary*, under "holiness," https://www.merriam-webster.com/dictionary/holiness.

11. Justin Giboney, "Forum on Cultural Engagement," YouTube, posted by Ozark Christian College, March 12, 2024, https://www.youtube.com/watch?v=7s-53QpjoBQ.

12. Giboney, "Forum on Cultural Engagement."

13. Russell Moore, host, *The Russell Moore Show*, podcast, episode 115, "James Davison Hunter on Challenges to Democracy," *Christianity Today*, July

17, 2024, https://www.russellmoore.com/2024/07/17/james-davison-hunter-on-challenges-to-democracy/.

14. Michael Wear, *The Spirit of Our Politics* (Zondervan, 2024), 212.

Chapter 14 Already, Not Yet

1. "*The Benedict Option*," Penguin Random House, accessed April 7, 2025, https://www.penguinrandomhouse.com/books/547188/the-benedict-option-by-rod-dreher/.

2. Eric Carle, *Pancakes, Pancakes!* (Picture Book Studio, 1992).

3. Nancy S. Love, "Shield Maidens, Fashy Femmes, and TradWives: Feminism, Patriarchy, and Right-Wing Populism," *Frontiers in Sociology* 5 (December 22, 2020), https://www.frontiersin.org/journals/sociology/articles/10.3389/fsoc.2020.619572/full.

4. Sophie Elmhirst, "The Rise and Fall of the Trad Wife," *The New Yorker*, March 29, 2024, https://www.newyorker.com/culture/persons-of-interest/the-rise-and-fall-of-the-trad-wife.

5. Elmhirst, "Rise and Fall of the Trad Wife."

6. Emma Green, "The Rebirth of America's Pro-Natalist Movement," *The Atlantic*, December 6, 2017, https://www.theatlantic.com/politics/archive/2017/12/pro-natalism/547493/.

7. Green, "Rebirth of America's Pro-Natalist Movement."

8. Love, "Shield Maidens."

9. Emma Beddington, "Sometimes I Long for the Life of a Tradwife. Then I Remember It's a Reactionary Fantasy," *The Guardian*, February 4, 2024, https://www.theguardian.com/commentisfree/2024/feb/04/sometimes-i-long-for-the-life-of-a-tradwife-then-i-remember-its-a-reactionary-fantasy.

10. Emma Cieslik, "Catholic Trad Wives Pose a Formidable Political and Religious Force," *National Catholic Reporter*, May 17, 2024, https://www.ncronline.org/opinion/guest-voices/catholic-trad-wives-pose-formidable-political-and-religious-force.

11. Ezra Klein, "MAGA's Big Tech Divide," *New York Times*, January 28, 2025, https://www.nytimes.com/2025/01/28/opinion/ezra-klein-podcast-james-pogue.html.

12. Willard, "Spiritual Formation."

13. Willard, "Spiritual Formation."

14. Jen Pollock Michel, "Desire as Paradox," *A Habit Called Faith* (blog), June 10, 2024, https://jenpollockmichel.substack.com/p/desire-as-paradox.

15. Pollock Michel, "Desire as Paradox."

Chapter 15 Evangelical Anxiety

1.Talique Taylor, "Why I'm Not an 'Exvangelical,'" *The Liberator* (blog), July 29, 2023, https://taliquethewriter.substack.com/p/why-im-not-an-exvangelical.

2. Alex Morris, "'An Evangelical Childhood Is a Total Mindf#$@': New Memoir Recounts the Anxiety and Thrills of Growing Up a Conservative Christian," *Rolling Stone*, June 18, 2022, https://www.rollingstone.com/culture/culture-features/evangelical-christians-1370190/.

3. Ruth Graham, "Piety and Profanity: The Raunchy Christians Are Here," *New York Times*, March 17, 2024, https://www.nytimes.com/2024/03/17/us/evangelicals-christians-conservative-trump.html.

4. Graham, "Piety and Profanity."

5. Graham, "Piety and Profanity."

6. Michael C. Bender, "The Church of Trump: How He's Infusing Christianity into His Movement," *New York Times*, April 1, 2024, https://www.nytimes.com/2024/04/01/us/politics/trump-2024-religion.html.

7. Dederer, *Monsters*, 122.

Chapter 16 Holy Indifference

1. "St. Ignatius's 14 Rules: In Our Language," accessed November 27, 2024, https://uploads.weconnect.com/mce/17e89c359872f5659b5d7892ba8e52821c93eef3/Revive/Simplified%20Rules%20of%20Ignatius.pdf.

2. "14 Rules for the Discernment of Spirits by St. Ignatius of Loyola," Scepter, August 3, 2018, https://scepterpublishers.org/blogs/scepter-blog-corner/14-rules-for-the-discernment-of-spirits-by-st-ignatius-of loyola.

3. "14 Rules for the Discernment of Spirits."

4. Merton and Kidd, *New Seeds of Contemplation*, 37.

5. Dale Gish, "The Contemplation of Divine Love 'The Contemplatio,'" unpublished manuscript, no date.

6. Gish, "Contemplation of Divine Love."

7. Marina Berzins McCoy, "Ignatian Indifference," Ignatian Spirituality, accessed March 6, 2025, https://www.ignatianspirituality.com/ignatian-indifference/, emphasis original.

8. Gish, "Contemplation of Divine Love."

9. Gish, "Contemplation of Divine Love."

10. Norris, *Amazing Grace*, 29.

11. Norris, *Amazing Grace*, 37.

12. Simone Weil, "Detachment," accessed November 27, 2024, https://rohandrape.net/ut/rttcc-text/Detachment.pdf.

13. Rainer Maria Rilke, *Letters to a Young Poet*, trans. M.D. Herter Norton (W.W. Norton & Company, 1993), 32.

14. Gish, "Contemplation of Divine Love."

SARA BILLUPS is a writer and cultural commentator with bylines in publications including *The New York Times* and *Christianity Today*. Sara holds a Doctor of Ministry in the Sacred Art of Writing from the Eugene Peterson Center for Christian Imagination at Western Theological Seminary. Sara writes *Bitter Scroll* on Substack and cohosts the podcast *That's the Spirit*. She lives in Seattle.

CONNECT WITH SARA

SaraBillups.com

 @Sara.Billups